Margaret Cavendish

The Female Academy

Recent Books by Sharon L. Jansen

Margaret Cavendish: The Convent of Pleasure. Saltar's Point Press, 2016.

Mary Astell: Some Reflections upon Marriage. Saltar's Point Press, 2014.

Mary Astell: A Serious Proposal to the Ladies. Saltar's Point Press, 2014.

Anne of France: "Lessons for My Daughter." The Library of Medieval Women. Boydell & Brewer, 2012.

Reading Women's Worlds from Christine de Pizan to Doris Lessing: A Guide to Six Centuries of Women Writers Imagining Rooms of Their Own. Palgrave Macmillan, 2011.

The Monstrous Regiment of Women: Female Rule in Early Modern Europe. Queenship and Power, ed. Carole Levin and Charles Beem. Palgrave Macmillan, 2010.

Debating Women, Politics, and Power in Early Modern Europe. Palgrave Macmillan, 2008.

Margaret Cavendish

The Female Academy

Edited by

Sharon L. Jansen

Saltar's
Point
Press

Margaret Cavendish, *The Female Academy*, edited by Sharon L. Jansen
Copyright © Sharon L. Jansen, 2017

First published 2017 by
Saltar's Point Press,
dedicated to producing
quality teaching texts for classroom use.

ISBN-13: 978-0692853238
ISBN-10: 0692853235

Grateful acknowledgment is made to the National Portrait Gallery (London) for permission to reproduce the frontispiece from Margaret Cavendish's *Playes* (London, 1662).

Grateful acknowledgement is made to Tagul (https://tagul.com) for its commercial licence permitting use of the word cloud generated through its web service as cover art for this book.

"A woman write a play! Out upon it, out upon it, for it cannot be good. Besides you say she is a lady, which is the likelier to make the play worse. A woman and a lady to write a play? Fie, fie!"

Margaret Cavendish, "Introduction," *Playes* (1662)

Contents

List of Figures   vii

Acknowledgments   viii

Introduction   1

   Margaret Cavendish's Life and Work   10

   Women, Performance, and Playwriting
     in Early-Modern England   31

   Margaret Cavendish and the Folio Tradition   54

   Margaret Cavendish's *The Female Academy* (1662)   66

   The Legacy of Margaret Cavendish and Her Work   76

   A Note on the Text   102

The Text of *The Female Academy*   107

Select Bibliography   155

Appendix: A Brief Chronology of Margaret Cavendish's
   Published Work   165

List of Figures

Figure 1.
   Frontispiece from *Playes*, "written by the thrice noble,
   illustrious and excellent princess, the lady marchioness
   of Newcastle" (London, 1662)   64

Figure 2.
   Title page from *Playes*, "written by the thrice noble,
   illustrious, and excellent princess, the lady marchioness
   of Newcastle" (London, 1662)   65

Acknowledgments

This edition of Margaret Cavendish's *The Female Academy* began with my transcription of the text from a copy of the 1662 *Playes* now held in the British Library. I have enjoyed reading a number of Cavendish's plays, including this one, with many students, and their responses to her and her work have contributed to this edition of *The Female Academy*: their engagement with her plays encouraged me to prepare classroom editions for them, their puzzlement over some of Cavendish's language indicated where they needed clarifications, definitions, and explanations, and their overwhelming enthusiasm and delight led to the present volume. I owe them my deepest thanks.

Today many readers can access the full text of *The Female Academy* through the Early English Books Online (EEBO) database. For those with library access, the play is also available through the English Prose Drama: The Full-Text Database (Chadwyck-Healey) and through the Women Writers Online full-text collection of early women's writing in English (Women Writers Project, Northeastern University).

This Saltar's Point Press edition of *The Female Academy* offers the text of the play in a single affordable volume. The introduction surveys Cavendish's life and work in the context of women's performance and playwriting in early-modern England. The text has been carefully edited and modernized, offering the reader ample notes and aids. The volume is completed by a bibliography with suggestions for further reading and a chronology of Margaret Cavendish's published work.

Introduction

Many readers first encounter Margaret Cavendish in the pages of Virginia Woolf's *A Room of One's One*. There, after her discussion of the fictional Shakespeare's sister, Woolf turns her attention to several early-modern women writers, Cavendish among them. Woolf's assessment is memorable. "What a vision of loneliness and riot the thought of Margaret Cavendish brings to mind!" Woolf exclaims, "as if some giant cucumber had spread itself over all the roses and carnations in the garden and choked them to death." Woolf acknowledges Cavendish's "passion for poetry" but concludes that her writing is "disfigured and deformed." Disfigured and deformed by her "rage," disfigured and deformed because "no one taught her."[1]

Cavendish was keenly aware of the deficiencies of her education. She would later write that she "never went to school" but "only learned to read and write at home," where she was "taught by an ancient decayed gentlewoman" who was "kept for that purpose."[2] Beyond those basic skills, the young Margaret was provided with lessons in singing, dancing, music, and needlework but, as she concedes, these were arranged "rather for formality than for benefit."[3] Even so, she claims to have been

---

[1] Virginia Woolf, *A Room of One's Own* (1929; rpt. New York: Harcourt / Harvest Edition, 1989), 61-62.

Portions of this introduction are adapted from the Introduction to Cavendish's *The Convent of Pleasure*, ed. Sharon L. Jansen (Saltar's Point Press, 2016).

[2] Margaret Cavendish, Letter 175, *CCXI Sociable Letters* (London, 1664), 367. I have silently modernized the spelling and punctuation.

[3] Margaret Cavendish (1623-1673) published an account of her life, *A True Relation of my Birth, Breeding and Life*, as the eleventh and final book in her *Natures Pictures Drawn by Fancies Pencil to the Life . . .* (London, 1656). In the second edition of *Natures Pictures* (London, 1671), *A True Relation* was omitted. Cavendish's autobiography is included in Charles H. Firth, ed., *The Life of William Cavendish, Duke of Newcastle, to which is added "The True Relation of My Birth Breeding and Life" by Margaret, Duchess of Newcastle*, 2nd rev. ed.,

something of reader when she was a child; though her "study of books" may have been "little," she still "chose rather to read" than to spend her time "in any other work or practice."[4] She also loved to write, and she later describes the way she filled sixteen "little baby-books" with her scribbles and blots. The contents were "as confused as the chaos, wherein is neither method nor order, but all mixed together without separation."[5] Still, however much she may have enjoyed reading and filling up pages with her "sense and no sense," the time she spent with "serious study" was limited, she confesses, "by reason that I took great delight in attiring, fine dressing, and fashions, especially such fashions as I did devise myself."[6]

Cavendish claims to have read and reread the plays of Shakespeare when she was a girl and reports that "going to plays" in London was among the "harmless recreations" enjoyed by female members of her family.[7] But while she might have enjoyed going to the theater with her mother and sisters, there was no role for women in the theater. The "golden age" of English drama glittered and shone for men only. Thousands of men and women attended performances at the London playhouses each week during the early seventeenth century, but they never heard a single word of dialogue spoken by a woman much less written by a woman: women did not perform on stage in the public theaters, nor did they write any of the plays that were acted there.[8] A very few aristocratic women translated dramatic texts, even fewer attempted to write an original comedy or tragedy—but no early-modern woman

---

(New York: E. P. Dutton, 1907). The quotation is from pp. 157-58. I have silently modernized the spelling and punctuation.

[4] Cavendish, *True Relation*, in Firth, ed., *Life of William Cavendish*, 175. I have silently modernized the spelling and punctuation.

[5] Margaret Cavendish, Letter 131, *Sociable Letters*, 267. I have silently modernized the spelling and punctuation.

[6] Cavendish, *True Relation*, in Firth, ed., *Life of William Cavendish*, 175. I have silently modernized the spelling and punctuation.

[7] On her love for Shakespeare when she was a "very young maid," see Cavendish, Letter 123 and Letter 162, *Sociable Letters*, 244-48 and 338-39, for example; on the Lucas family's attending the theater in London, see Cavendish, *A True Relation*, in Firth, ed., *Life of William Cavendish*, 159-60. I have silently modernized the spelling and punctuation.

[8] According to theater historian Tanya Pollard, "up to twenty-five thousand people attended theatrical performances in London each week between 1580 and 1640." Pollard, ed., *Shakespeare's Theater: A Sourcebook* (Malden, MA: Blackwell, 2004), xii.

writer could ever hope to see her play acted on the English stage.[9] And if writing a play was difficult and performance impossible, publication was just as problematic for women writers. Publication—public speech—violated gender ideologies that expected women to be chaste, silent, and obedient. Finally, as if all these obstacles were not enough for her when she eventually made the decision to write and publish plays, Margaret Cavendish faced another difficulty after the outbreak of the English Civil Wars: in 1642, the great London playhouses were closed by order of parliament.[10]

Limited by her education and sex, stung by criticisms of her intellectual ambitions, and knowing that professional theaters had been closed in England, Margaret Cavendish nevertheless began writing plays, both comedies and tragedies, at some point in the 1650s. By the time she published her first collection of dramatic work in 1662, the world had changed, once again, for English playwrights, performers, and audiences—in August of 1660, just weeks after Charles II landed in England, the new Stuart king, now restored to the throne, reopened the theaters under a royal charter, offering patents to two dramatic companies, the King's Company, under the management of the dramatist Thomas Killigrew, and the Duke's Company, managed by the poet and playwright William Davenant. Among the many theatrical innovations Killigrew and Davenant introduced, one was remarkable: for the first time, Englishwomen began to act on the public stage.[11] But the possibilities for Margaret Cavendish as a woman writing drama were still limited. Despite the obstacles, she dared to offer a second volume, *Plays, Never before Printed*, in 1668.

While Margaret Cavendish was not the first Englishwoman to write a play or to publish one, she was first woman to present her dramatic work in a folio collection. As critic Shannon Miller observes, the production

---

[9] On the difficulties for women writing drama in the generation before Cavendish, see Marion Wynne-Davies, "The Theater," in *The History of British Women's Writing*, vol. 2, *1500-1610*, ed. Caroline Bicks and Jennifer Summit, The History of British Women's Writing (New York: Palgrave Macmillan, 2010), 175-95. On the very few early-modern women writers of dramatic texts in England, see below, 39-49.

[10] An Ordinance concerning Stage Plays, 2 September 1642. In *Acts and Ordinances of the Interregnum, 1642-1660*, ed. C. H. Firth and R. S. Rait (London: His Majesty's Stationery Office, 1911), 26-27.

[11] For a discussion of women, performance, and the English stage before 1660, see below, 31-39.

of such folio volumes was crucial to the "emerging seventeenth-century canonical hierarchy of playwrights" and "central in establishing reputations."[12] The playwright Ben Jonson was the first to publish a folio edition of his dramatic work in his 1616 *The Works of Benjamin Johnson*.[13] This was followed in 1623 by *Mr. William Shakespeare's Comedies, Histories, and Tragedies, Published According to the True Original Copies*, an edition now commonly referred to as the "First Folio"; in 1632 by the Second Folio of Shakespeare; in 1640 by a second edition of Jonson's *Works*; and in 1647 by the publication of the *Comedies and Tragedies Written by Francis Beaumont and John Fletcher, Gentlemen, Never Printed before, and Now Published by the Authors' Original Copies*. Into the midst of this dramatic print contest, Cavendish wedged herself and her two folio volumes, the 1662 *Plays* and the 1668 *Plays, Never before Printed*. But, as Jeffrey Masten notes, such large-format publications constituted a "theatrical discourse perceived as conversation between men." A "woman's entrance" into this territory was both "treacherous and heavily policed," and neither one of Cavendish's folios appeared in a second edition.[14] Meanwhile, the works of male playwrights continued to appear with mind-numbing regularity: a Third Folio of Shakespeare's work in 1663, a second folio of Beaumont and Fletcher, titled *Fifty Comedies and Tragedies*, in 1679, a Shakespeare Fourth Folio in 1685, a third edition of the Jonson's *Works* in 1692. Even

---

[12] Miller, "'Thou art a Moniment, without a tombe': Affiliation and Memorialization in Margaret Cavendish's *Playes* and *Plays, Never before Printed*," in *Cavendish and Shakespeare, Interconnections*, ed. Katherine Romack and James Fitzmaurice (Burlington, VT: Ashgate Publishing, 2006), 9. The term "folio" refers to the size of the book, in this case a large volume in which the sheet of paper has been folded only once (producing two leaves and four pages), as opposed to the quarto volume, with the sheet folded twice (producing four leaves and eight pages), and the octavo, with the sheet folded three times (producing eight leaves and sixteen pages).

[13] Before Jonson's use of the folio for his *Works*, play texts were printed in quarto and octavo formats. As Lynne S. Meskill notes, "Folios were large, unwieldy, expensive and luxurious. They were destined for aristocrats, the rich, the learned; smaller formats were akin to pamphlets: cheap, easily available and widely disseminated." By contrast, the folio format "was reserved for serious literature: namely epic and poetry and serious readers, possessors of libraries and reading lecterns." Jonson's decision to print his plays in this format was thus a "revolutionary" act, "with its implicit assertion" that dramatic work was also "serious literature." Meskill, "Ben Jonson's 1616 Folio: A Revolution in Print?" *Études Épistémè* 14 (2008): 179.

[14] Masten, *Textual Intercourse: Collaboration, Authorship, and Sexualities in Renaissance Drama* (New York: Cambridge University Press, 1997), 120, 156. For more on Cavendish's use of the folio format for her plays, see below, 54–63.

today, well into the second decade of the twenty-first century and more than 350 years after Cavendish dared to publish two collections of her plays, her folios have never been republished. For Margaret Cavendish there were no second acts.

But that should not surprise us.

Today, in many parts of the world, but most particularly in North America and western Europe, significant numbers of women have made undeniable progress in their effort to achieve equality. And yet, despite the undeniable progress that has been made, women's participation in many areas of society remains limited—women are under-represented in politics and government, in business and technology, and in far too many professions, and they still suffer economic disparity simply because they are female. Nowhere do we see this gender gap more clearly than in the field where Margaret Cavendish sought a place among her male contemporaries. Whether their professional careers are in theater, film, or television, women are still not equal participants.

In commenting on the opportunities for women in theatrical productions, playwright Marsha Norman recently noted, "Women have lived half of the experience of the world, but only 20 percent of it is recorded in our theatres."[15] In a comprehensive study of 153 U.S. theaters, published in 2015, the Dramatists Guild of America reported that only 22 percent of the plays produced in a three-year period were by women writers. In other words, "if life worked like the theatre, four out of five things you had ever heard would have been said by men."[16] Onstage and back stage, there is also a colossal gender gap: significantly fewer roles for female actors than male, and noticeably fewer female directors, set designers, lighting designers, sound designers, and choreographers, among other crucial roles.[17] As a recent study on gender

---

[15] Quoted in Suzy Evans, "The Gender Parity Count Ticks Up—Slightly," *American Theater*, 20 July 2015, http://www.americantheatre.org/2015/07/20/the-gender-parity-count-ticks-up-slightly/.

[16] Marsha Norman, "Why 'The Count' Matters," *The Dramatist* 18, no. 2 (2015): 18. The study covered three consecutive seasons, 2011-12, 2012-13, and 2013-14. For the methodology used in the study, see pp. 20-21. A complete list of "all the theaters counted" is found on p. 29.

[17] See Suzy Evans, "Women Push for Equality On and Off Stage," *American Theatre*, October 2014, http://www.americantheatre.org/2014/09/17/women-push-for-equality-on-and-off-stage/; Martha Wade Steketee and Judith Binus, *Women Count:*

equality in performing arts in the UK recently concluded, "When it comes to what audiences see and hear on stage, it remains overwhelmingly written, directed, designed and performed by men."[18]

At the same time, on screens both large and small, women face similar inequities.[19] Recent studies of the top 100 films released in 2016 reveal women accounted for only 11 percent of the writers, 4 percent of the directors, 19 percent of the producers, 14 percent of the editors, and 3 percent of the cinematographers.[20] On screen, women accounted for only 31.4 percent of "speaking or named characters" in the top 100 films of 2015—moreover, in these one hundred films, only 5 women over the age of forty-five "performed a lead or co lead role."[21] (And, of course, the characters played by women in these movies were "three times as likely as their male counterparts to be shown in sexually revealing

---

Women Hired Off-Broadway 2010-2015 (New York: League of Professional Theatre Women, 2015), http://theatrewomen.org/women-count/; and Gordon Cox, "When Will Broadway's Onstage Diversity Carry Over Behind the Curtain?" *Variety*, 10 November 2015, http://variety.com/2015/biz/features/broadway-diversity-behind-the-scenes-1201636823/. For a similar analysis of theaters on the West Coast, see, for example, Valerie Weak, *Not Even: A Gender Analysis of 500 San Francisco/Bay Area Theatrical Productions from the Counting Actors Project, 2011-2014* (San Francisco: Women Arts, 2015), http://www.womenarts.org/not-even/.

For a brief overview of the issues in Canada, see Yvette HeyLiger's report on the Equity Theatre Symposium in Canada, *The Dramatist* 18, no. 2 (2015): 48-50.

[18] Tonic Theatre, "What We Learned," *Advance: Gender Equality in England's Theatres* (September 2014), http://www.tonictheatre-advance.co.uk/advance-2014/why/.

[19] For a comprehensive study of women in both film and television, see Stacy L. Smith et al., *Inclusion or Invisibility? Comprehensive Annenberg Report on Diversity in Entertainment* (Los Angeles: USC Annenberg School for Communication and Journalism's Media, Diversity, & Social Change Initiative, 2016).

[20] For these figures, see Martha M. Lauzen, *The Celluloid Ceiling: Behind-the-Scenes Employment of Women on the Top 100, 250, and 500 Films of 2016* (San Diego: Center for the Study of Women in Television and Film, 2017), 4. Overall, these figures represent a decline from 2015—and, even more depressing, they are "even with the percentage achieved in 1993," 1.

[21] Stacy L. Smith et al., "Key Findings," *Inequality in 800 Popular Films: Examining Portrayals of Gender, Race/Ethnicity, LGBT, and Disability from 2007 to 2015* (Los Angeles: USC Annenberg School for Communication and Journalism's Media, Diversity, & Social Change Initiative, 2016), 1. In addition to this longitudinal study, see Martha M. Lauzen, *It's a Man's (Celluloid) World: On-Screen Representations of Female Characters in the Top 100 Films of 2014* (San Diego: Center for the Study of Women in Television and Film, 2015).

clothing."[22] No do these numbers address the issue of pay equity.[23] While women are more fully represented on television screens than they are in film—in the 2015-16 prime-time season, 38 percent of the "major characters" on broadcast, cable, and Netflix programs were female—they still comprised only 27 percent of the writers, 11 percent of the directors, 36 percent of the producers, 22 percent of editors, and 3 percent of directors of photography, among other roles.[24]

As Stacy Smith concludes in her study of the portrayals of women in film, inequality is "startling and consistent," and it remains "an industry norm": "despite advocacy and good intentions, change remains difficult to achieve."[25] Or, as Martha Lauzen, director of the Center for the Study of Women in Television and Film, says, more succinctly, when it comes to the big screen, women still encounter a "celluloid ceiling." And on the small screen, it's much the same: women are, even now, "boxed in."

Virginia Woolf's description of Margaret Cavendish in *A Room of One's Own* is both memorable and memorably horrifying. But those comments were a kind of second draft for Woolf—she had first written at some length about Cavendish a few years earlier. In *The Common Reader*, a collection of essays and reviews published in 1925, Woolf reveals that she is familiar not only with Cavendish's biography of her husband, William Cavendish, but also with her *Poems and Fancies*, her "female orations" and "philosophical letters," and her plays. "[H]er poems, her plays, her philosophies, her orations, her discourses," Woolf writes, "all those folios and quartos in which, she protested, her real life was shrined—moulder in the gloom of public libraries, or are decanted into tiny thimbles which hold six drops of their profusion."[26]

In this essay Woolf is more nuanced about Cavendish. Not that Woolf is unabashedly glowing in her praises of Cavendish, but neither

---

[22] Smith et al., "Key Findings," *Inequality in 800 Films*, 1.

[23] On pay equity for film actors, see Ramin Setoodeh, "Equal Pay Revolution: How Top Actresses Are Finally Fighting Back," *Variety*, 10 November 2015, http://variety.com/2015/film/news/hollywood-gender-pay-gap-inequality-01636553/.

[24] Martha M. Lauzen, *Boxed In: Women On Screen and Behind the Scenes in Television, 2015-16* (San Diego: Center for the Study of Women in Television and Film, 2016), 13, 15.

[25] Smith et al., *Inequality in 800 Films*, 25.

[26] Woolf, *The Common Reader, First Series* (1925; rpt. New York: Houghton Mifflin /Mariner Books, 2002), 69.

does she condemn her with that terrible image, the ugly cucumber vine smothering the roses and carnations. Woolf seems to appreciate the "wild streak" in Cavendish that was "forever upsetting the orderly arrangements of nature," and she is quite clear about the reasons why Cavendish drew upon herself such heaps of public "ridicule." "People were censorious," Woolf observes, "men were jealous of brains in a woman; women suspected intellect in their own sex."[27] Though "her philosophies are futile, and her plays intolerable, and her verses mainly dull," Woolf can't quite resist or dismiss Margaret Cavendish: "One cannot help following the lure of her erratic and lovable personality as it meanders and twinkles through page after page. There is something noble and Quixotic and high-spirited, as well as crack-brained and bird-witted, about her." Despite everything, "the vast bulk of the duchess is leavened by a vein of authentic fire."[28]

Despite the spark of this "authentic fire," as Woolf observes, Cavendish's "terrible" critics "sneered and jeered" at her, and these "tormentors," who could little appreciate her ambition, much less her accomplishments, "mocked her." For her part, Cavendish claimed to disregard all the criticism and ridicule. When she dared to publish her second collection of plays in 1668, for example, she brushed her critics aside, declaring, "I write . . . only for my own pleasure and not to please others." Well aware of her "envious detractors," she was defiant: "malice cannot hinder me from writing, wherein consists my chiefest delight and greatest pastime." She insisted that she would continue to publish her books regardless of whether "anybody reads them or not" and that, in any case, she wasn't writing for her contemporaries: "I regard not so much the present as future ages, for which I intend all my books," adding that, if future readers liked her work, that was all that mattered.[29]

The future readers that Cavendish once imagined—or hoped for— have at long last emerged, and the "terrible" critics and "tormentors" who loved to sneer and jeer at her work are no longer mocking her. Today the International Margaret Cavendish Society has members in the UK, the US, Canada, Australia, New Zealand, France, Italy, Germany, Greece, the Netherlands, Norway, Portugal, India, Israel, and Japan.

---

[27] Woolf, *The Common Reader*, 71.

[28] Woolf, *The Common Reader*, 77.

[29] Margaret Cavendish, "To the Reader," *Plays, Never before Printed* (London, 1668), A1r. I have silently modernized the spelling and punctuation.

Panel discussions at scholarly conferences explore Cavendish's contributions to literature, philosophy, political theory, economics, medicine, science, gender and sexuality studies, and ecofeminism. Cavendish's work is debated and analyzed in the pages of academic articles and in college classrooms, but she's equally at home online—you'll find Margaret Cavendish at the Poetry Foundation website, for example, and she's also a popular figure at sites dedicated to science fiction and fantasy.[30]

While there is still no independent entry for Margaret Cavendish in the *Encyclopedia Britannica* (she is briefly mentioned in the "Women in Science" article), her work has found its way into standard literature anthologies and reference sources like the *Norton Anthology of Literature* and the *Stanford Encyclopedia of Philosophy*. There is also a lively Cavendish presence in popular culture: a graphic novel, *Mad Madge*, in the Dawn of the Unread series; a place in *Shape and Situate: Posters of Inspirational Women in Europe*, dedicated to "remembering who we are"; an episode in the *Stuff Mom Never Told You* podcast; and dozens of YouTube videos and Prezi presentations, most of them created and posted by students from all over the world.[31]

Cavendish has also proved to be a source of inspiration for contemporary novelists. In 2014, Siri Hustvedt's *The Blazing World* was long-listed for the Man Booker Prize—the novel not only borrows its title from Cavendish's utopian fantasy, published in 1666, but Cavendish

[30] Ro Smith, "Reviewing through the Time Machine: Remembering Margaret Cavendish" (*The Rhubosphere Blog*, 17 July 2012, http://rhube.co.uk/wp/2012/07/17/reviewing-through-the-time-machine-remembering-margaret-cavendish/), reprinted in *Speculative Fiction 2012: The Best Online Reviews, Essays, and Commentary*, ed. Justin Landon and Jared Shurin (London: Jurassic, 2013); this anthology won the British Fantasy Award for Non-Fiction in 2014. In 2015, the online quarterly *Holdfast* won the British Fantasy Society Best Magazine Award; Hel Gurney's "Margaret Cavendish: Science Fiction and Fantasy's Forgotten Ancestress" is in the first issue (http://www.holdfast-magazine.com/margaret-cavendish-nf1/4579796779).

[31] The *Mad Madge* graphic novel, written by Mhairi Stewart and illustrated by Gary Erskine, is issue 15 (2015) of the Dawn of the Dead series ("When the dead go unread there's gonna be trouble"), produced by Nottingham Trent University, available online at http://www.dawnoftheunread.com/issue-15-01.html. Anne-Marie Atkinson's Cavendish poster is in *Shape and Situate*, issue 5 (2013), http://remember-who-u-are.blogspot.co.uk/p/shape-situate-posters-of-inspirational.html. Margaret Cavendish is included in the "Empresses of Science Fiction" episode, *Stuff Mom Never Told You* (6 July 2015), http://www.stuffmomnevertoldyou.com/podcasts/empresses-of-science-fiction/.

herself appears as an "alter ego" for Hustvedt's main character, Harriet
Burden. "I am a Riot. An Opera. A Menace," Harriet says, calling
Cavendish "my blazing mother Margaret," she who "gives birth to
worlds." Critic Jonathon Sturgeon recently named Danielle Dutton's
"anti-historical historical novel," *Margaret the First,* as one of the "50 most
anticipated books of 2016."[32]

In ways Virginia Woolf could never have imagined, Margaret
Cavendish has gained the appreciative readers she once imagined for
herself. She may also have anticipated her current status as something of
a feminist icon. In a letter addressed to "the two universities" of Oxford
and Cambridge published in her *Philosophical and Physical Opinions,* she
offers up to them her work not in the hope that such "wise schoolmen
and industrious, laborious students should value [her] book for any
worth," but that they might be gracious enough to "receive it without
scorn for the good encouragement of [her] sex." She hopes these "most
famously learned" men will treat her with a "respectful civility"—but if
this "sage society" decides instead to "bury" her in "silence," she claims
she will be satisfied with her "quiet grave." Lying "entombed under the
dust of a university will be honor enough," she says. And yet . . . Even if
she is ignored by the professors of the "two famous universities" and
"buried" by scholarly men who choose to ignore her, she slyly asks, "who
knows?" Her "honorable burial" may after all prove "a glorious
resurrection in following ages, since time brings strange and unusual
things to pass."[33]

The "resurrection" of Cavendish's life and work today, some three
and a half centuries after her death, has vindicated her prophecy.
"Strange and unusual things" have indeed come to pass for Margaret
Cavendish.

Margaret Cavendish's Life and Work

Born in 1623, Margaret Cavendish began life as Margaret Lucas,
youngest of the eight children of Sir Thomas Lucas and his wife,

---

[32] Siri Hustvedt, *The Blazing World* (New York: Simon & Schuster, 2014), 6 and 328.
For Sturgeon's comments, see "The 50 Most Anticipated Books of 2016," *Flavorwire* (5
January 2016), http://flavorwire.com/554364/the-50-most-anticipated-books-of-
2016/25.

[33] "To the Two Universities," *The Philosophical and Physical Opinions* (London, 1655),
n. p.

Elizabeth Leighton. Although her father was not a "peer of the realm," Cavendish was proud of her family's status: "My father was a gentleman, which title is grounded and given by merit, not by princes."[34] The Lucas family lived comfortably and happily at St. John's Abbey, their estate near Colchester, and managed to maintain their affluent style of life even after Thomas Lucas's death in 1625 when Margaret was, in her own words, still "an infant."[35] The Lucas estate was necessarily divided between Thomas Lucas's sons and his wife, as Cavendish notes in her autobiography, but Elizabeth Lucas did not suffer the kind of economic loss so many women in her situation faced; since the widow and her children "agreed with a mutual consent," Margaret writes, "all their affairs were managed so well as she lived not in a much lower condition than when my father lived."[36]

---

[34] Cavendish, *True Relation*, in Firth, ed., *Life of William Cavendish*, 155. I have silently modernized the spelling and punctuation. In addition to her autobiography, there are four principal accounts of Margaret Lucas Cavendish's life: Douglas Grant, *Margaret the First: A Biography of Margaret Cavendish, Duchess of Newcastle, 1623-1675* (London: Rupert Hart-Davis, 1957); Kathleen Jones, *A Glorious Fame: The Life of Margaret Cavendish, Duchess of Newcastle, 1623-1673* (London: Bloomsbury Publishing, 1988); Katie Whitaker, *Mad Madge: The Extraordinary Life of Margaret Cavendish, Duchess of Newcastle, the First Woman to Live by Her Pen* (New York: Basic Books, 2002); and James Fitzmaurice, "Cavendish, Margaret, duchess of Newcastle upon Tyne (1623?-1673)," *Oxford Dictionary of National Biography* [online] (Oxford: Oxford University Press, 2004-), http://oxforddnb.com.

[35] Cavendish, *True Relation*, in Firth, ed., *Life of William Cavendish*, 156. I have silently modernized the spelling and punctuation.

Elizabeth Leighton was pregnant with her first child in the summer of 1597, although she and Sir Thomas Lucas were not married, a fact Cavendish omits in *A True Relation*. Cavendish does, however, reveal that her father killed Sir William Brooke—adding, in his defense, that her father was compelled, "in honor" to challenge Brooke and "in justice" killed him (155). Declared an outlaw, Sir Thomas fled to the continent, where he remained until after Queen Elizabeth's death in 1603. Lucas was ultimately pardoned by James I, and on 18 March 1604, the new king issued a warrant restoring him to his status and property. Only then could Sir Thomas Lucas return home—his eldest son, named for his father, was by that time six years old. Sir Thomas married Elizabeth Leighton in 1604, but because of the circumstances of the younger Thomas's birth, the eldest Lucas son could not be his father's heir. A second son and heir, John, was born in 1606, followed by Mary (born c. 1608), Elizabeth (born c. 1612), Charles (b. 1613), Anne (b. c. 1614-16?), and Catherine (born 1617). Margaret's birth followed six years later, in 1623.

[36] Cavendish, *True Relation*, in Firth, ed., *Life of William Cavendish*, 156. I have silently modernized the spelling and punctuation.

The idyllic life of the Lucas family was disrupted after the outbreak of the English Civil Wars in 1642—Cavendish laments that her family was "ruined" by the "unhappy wars" descending on them "like a whirlwind," separating members of the family from one another, depriving them of their income, destroying their property, and taking the lives of far too many members of the close-knit family. At the very outset of the war, on 21 August 1642, while John Lucas, Margaret's older brother, was mustering troops for the royalist cause, St. John's Abbey was attacked by a huge crowd of men, women, and children from nearby Colchester; in addition to taking horses and armor, they seized "plate, money, books, boxes, writings and household stuff."[37] John Lucas was captured and transferred to a prison in London (he was released on bail in September and promptly joined the king's army); John's wife, Anne Neville, and his mother, Elizabeth, were threatened and held in the town jail. The crowd was still not satisfied. Throughout the next day, angry members of the town attacked the house itself, breaking windows and doors, destroying the gardens, pulling down fences, even killing livestock and deer.

It's not clear from surviving records whether Margaret, then about nineteen years old, was at St. John's Abbey when it was attacked, or whether she was in London at the home of her married sister, Catherine Lucas Pye. After being forced out of their home, members of the Lucas family eventually assembled in London and then relocated to Oxford, where Charles I had set up his court. The years of war that followed continued to be as devastating for the Lucases as the first few weeks of the conflict had been. Margaret's youngest brother, Charles, was captured in 1648 at the siege of Colchester, condemned for treason by a parliamentary court, and executed on 28 August 1648. Her eldest brother, Thomas, died of wounds he received in 1649. John Lucas was again captured and imprisoned in 1655. Nor were the Lucas women spared. Margaret lost her eldest sister, Mary Lucas Killigrew, in 1646, "her death being . . . hastened through grief of her only daughter," a little girl who had died of consumption six months earlier. Margaret's own mother, Elizabeth, died soon after Mary: "my mother lived to see the ruin of her children, in which was her ruin, and then died," Cavendish

---

[37] Contemporary accounts quoted in Grant, *Margaret the First*, 52.

writes.[38] As if all that were not enough, St. John's Abbey, which had been looted in 1642, was destroyed in the 1648 siege that ended with Charles Lucas's execution—heavily damaged by artillery bombardment during the siege, the abbey's destruction was complete when royalist munitions, stored inside, exploded. Finding nothing left to loot, the besieging troops broke open the Lucas family tomb in St. Giles's Church, on the abbey grounds, scattering the bones "with profane jests." The bodies of the recently buried Elizabeth Lucas and her daughter, Mary Killigrew, were still intact; the soldiers cut off the women's hair and wore it in their hats, a grim talisman of their victory.[39]

Meanwhile, in 1643, while she was with her family in Oxford, Margaret secured a place as lady-in-waiting to Queen Henrietta Maria, the French-born wife of King Charles I; when the queen fled the strife-torn country in 1644, Margaret Lucas left England with her. While the grieving and extremely shy Margaret was in Paris with the English court-in-exile, she met and married William Cavendish, a widower some thirty years her senior.[40] Having suffered a humiliating military defeat at the battle of Marston Moor—and despite the king's wishes—William Cavendish had fled England with his two sons and brother, living in Hamburg before joining English exiles in Paris. The young Margaret was noted for her bashfulness and her beauty, William for his wealth and his devotion to the royalist cause. After her marriage, Margaret began the education she had not had when she was a child. Her husband read to and with his young wife, engaged with her, challenged her, and fostered her interests in a broad range of topics, including politics, philosophy, literature, and science. She characterized herself as his "apprentice," adding that no one ever had "a more abler master to learn from than I have."[41]

---

[38] Cavendish, *True Relation*, in Firth, ed., *Life of William Cavendish*, 165. I have silently modernized the spelling and punctuation.

[39] Contemporary accounts quoted in Grant, *Margaret the First*, 101.

[40] William Cavendish (1592-1676) became the Viscount Mansfield in 1620, earl of Newcastle-upon-Tyne in 1628, marquess of Newcastle-upon Tyne in 1643, and first duke of Newcastle-upon-Tyne in 1665. He was the grandson of the formidable "Bess of Hardwick," Elizabeth Talbot, countess of Hardwick, whose second marriage (of four) had been to the Tudor courtier Sir William Cavendish (c. 1505-1557).

[41] Margaret Cavendish, *The Worlds Olio* (London, 1655), n. p. The passage is from the epistle between Book 1, part 1 and Book 1, part 2 (the last page in Book 1, part 1

Under her husband's tutelage, she began to write once more—even more daring, she would publish her work. Ambitious, inventive, and prolific, Margaret Cavendish knew the risks she was taking. In an introductory letter included in her first published book, she acknowledged the difficulties she faced as a writer: "I shall be censured by my own sex, and men will cast a smile of scorn upon my book because they think thereby women encroach too much upon their prerogatives, for they hold books as their crown and the sword as their scepter, by which they rule and govern." She was well aware of the virulent personal attacks that Mary Sidney Wroth had endured three decades earlier when she published her romance, *Urania*; Cavendish imagined that the reaction to her own efforts might be similar. Scornful male readers were likely to respond to her "as to the lady that wrote the *Romancy*, 'Work, lady, work, let writing books alone, / For surely wiser women ne'er wrote one.'"[42]

During the years of exile the couple endured, Margaret Cavendish's intellectual development was not only fostered by her husband, but she was also privileged to meet some of the greatest philosophers of her day,

---

is numbered 26; Book 1, part 2 begins on a page numbered 27). I have silently modernized the spelling and punctuation.

[42] Margaret Cavendish, "To All Noble, and Worthy Ladies," *Poems, and Fancies* (London, 1653), n. p. I have silently modernized the spelling and punctuation.

Cavendish is quoting Lord Edward Denny's scurrilous attack on Mary Wroth after the 1621 publication of *Urania*; Denny condemned Wroth as a "hermaphrodite in show, in deed a monster / As by thy words and works all men may conster." His twenty-six line poem ends, "leave idle books alone / For wise and worthier women have writte none." Quoted in *The Poems of Lady Mary Wroth*, ed. Josephine A. Roberts (Baton Rouge: Louisiana State University Press, 1983), 33. Denny's letter to Wroth was not published, but the verse must have circulated widely, since Roberts reports that "it appears in two seventeenth-century manuscripts." And, as Cavendish's reference makes clear, this bitter comment must still have concerned women writers more than thirty years after it was written. Cavendish alludes to this warning once again in the prefatory address to her husband, "To His Excellency the Lord Marquis of Newcastle," in *Sociable Letters* (1664): "It may be said to me, as one said to a Lady, *Work Lady, Work, let writing Books alone, For surely Wiser Women ne'r writ one*" (n. p.)

Although Mary Wroth's *Urania* had been published three decades before Cavendish published her *Poems, and Fancies*, James Fitzmaurice reminds us that, while "a great many respected women wrote and shared what they had written within coteries," Wroth was the "last woman of good birth to write for the press" before Cavendish began to publish her work, and Wroth's "fate was not to be envied." Fitzmaurice, "Fancy and the Family: Self-Characterizations of Margaret Cavendish," *Huntington Library Quarterly* 53, no. 3 (1990): 202.

including Thomas Hobbes and René Descartes. Yet Cavendish was keenly aware of how disadvantaged she was in making the acquaintance of these famous men and how ill equipped she was to profit from any intellectual exchange with them.

Thomas Hobbes had a long association with the Cavendish family— he had been the tutor of an earlier William Cavendish (our William's cousin). When he was still a young man, Margaret's husband had met Hobbes at the Cavendish family home, Welbeck Abbey, and William eventually became a great patron of the philosopher (Hobbes dedicated his 1640 *Elements of Law, Natural and Politic*, among other works, to William). In Paris, Hobbes frequently dined with William Cavendish, and so, Margaret writes, "I have had the like good fortune to see him."[43] But her interaction with the philosopher was limited: she never heard him discuss philosophy (though she does describe a conversation between Hobbes and her husband about witches), and, she claims, "I never spoke to Master Hobbes twenty words in my life."[44] Those twenty words must have included an invitation she extended to him to come to dinner: "I cannot say I did not ask him a question, for when I was in London, I . . . asked him if he would please to do me that honor to stay at dinner, but he with great civility refused me, as having some business, which I suppose required his absence." She read Hobbes's *Leviathan* when it was published in 1651, the same year she could finally read his 1642 *De cive*, published for the first time in an English translation.[45]

As for Descartes, who corresponded with the young William Cavendish and later debated with him while William was in exile in Paris, Margaret writes, "upon my conscience I never spoke to Mon-

---

[43] Cavendish, "An Epilogue to My Philosophical Opinions, *The Philosophical and Physical Opinions*, 2nd ed. (London, 1663), n. p. I have silently modernized the spelling and punctuation.

[44] Margaret Cavendish, *The Life of . . . William Cavendishe . . .* (London, 1667), 143-46; in Firth, ed., *Life of William Cavendish*, 106-108. I have silently modernized the spelling and punctuation.

[45] On Cavendish's reading of translations of Hobbes, see Whitaker, *Mad Madge*, 116. Recently, some scholars have argued that Cavendish was more familiar with Hobbes's work than previously believed. See, for example, Lisa Sarosahn, "Leviathan and the Lady: Cavendish's Critique of Hobbes in *The Philosophical Letters*," in *Authorial Conquests: Essays on Genre in the Writings of Margaret Cavendish*, ed. Line Cottegnies and Nancy Weitz (Madison, NJ: Fairleigh Dickinson University Press, 2003), 40-58, and L. E. Semler, "Margaret Cavendish's Early Engagement with Descartes and Hobbes: Philosophical Revisitation and Poetic Selection," *Intellectual History Review* 22, no. 3 (2012): 327-53.

sieur Descartes in my life, nor ever understood what he said, for he spoke no English, and I understand no other language, and those times I saw him, which was twice at dinner with my lord at Paris, he did appear to me a man of the fewest words I ever heard."[46] To read any part of Descartes's major works, including his *Principia philosophia* and his *Discours de la méthode*, she had to have sections translated for her into English.[47]

Thus, despite her avid interest in philosophy, politics, and government, Margaret Cavendish could not debate with men like Hobbes and Descartes even when she met them. She could only engage with their ideas textually—as she did in her 1664 *Philosophical Letters*.[48] There in a series of 157 letters, she is able to explore the philosophies of "several famous and learned authors," including Hobbes and Descartes. In this imagined correspondence, an unnamed female letter-writer sends questions to her "ladyship," soliciting her assistance in understanding the philosophical works she has been trying to read. "Cavendish" responds to her "humble and faithful servant" by addressing the reader's questions, outlining her critique of the philosophers' arguments and positions, and offering her own opinions and theories. Thus Cavendish can "debate" the ideas of men like Hobbes and Descartes in her epistles, but she can never engage the great men directly, either in person or in print.

In 1648, pressed by debts, the couple left Paris and moved to Antwerp, which William Cavendish judged to be "the most pleasantest and quietest place to retire himself and ruined fortunes in"; there Cavendish busied herself by writing about poetry, history, and drama, gathering her essays, reflections, poems, and opinions into a collection. But her work was interrupted in 1651 when, she writes, "necessity" forced her to return to England to "seek for relief." Learning that William Cavendish's forfeited estates were to be sold, the couple hoped that Margaret, as his wife, might be able to secure from parliament an "allowance" or "benefit" from the sale. Thus she traveled back to

---

[46] Cavendish, "An Epilogue to My Philosophical Opinions," *Philosophical and Physical Opinions*, n. p. I have silently modernized the spelling and punctuation.

[47] Whitaker, *Mad Madge*, 259.

[48] Margaret Cavendish, *Philosophical Letters, or, Modest Reflections upon Some Opinions in Natural Philosophy Maintained by Several Famous and Learned Authors of This Age, Expressed by Way of Letters* (London, 1664).

England with her brother-in-law, Charles Cavendish, aiming to secure some provision out of her husband's confiscated property.[49]

Before leaving, she put her writing aside, locking it up in a trunk "as if it had been buried in a grave."[50] Once in London, she found that her petition for support failed—it was denied because her husband was regarded as a traitor to the English state, and, as she was informed, she had married him knowing that his estate had been confiscated. Disappointed—the Cavendishes were living on credit, and debts were mounting—she met her husband's grown children for the first time and reunited with members of her own family, including her surviving sisters, Elizabeth Lucas Walter, Anne Lucas, and Catherine Lucas Pye, with her brother John and his wife Anne, and with her brother Thomas's widow, Anne Byron Lucas. But her visits otherwise were few (she says they numbered only "some half score"), and her entertainments even fewer (two or three musical evenings). She would later write that, during her time in London, she rarely left her lodgings even to "take the air" in Hyde Park with her sisters.

Anxious and deeply lonely, Cavendish turned once more to her pen. As her stay in England dragged on, she gathered her new compositions, including "poetical fictions, moral instructions, philosophical opinions, dialogues, discourses, [and] poetical romances," into a volume she would publish under the title of *Poems and Fancies*.[51] Even after sending her work to the printer, Cavendish continued writing, hoping to add additional material to the volume before it was published. Over the course of three weeks, she completed a series of philosophical essays on a wide range of topics, but as quickly as she wrote, it was not quick enough—the essays arrived too late to be included in *Poems and Fancies*, so they were published separately as *Philosophical Fancies*.[52]

---

[49] Cavendish describes her difficult and disappointing trip to England in *True Relation*, in Firth, ed., *Life of William Cavendish*, 166-70.

[50] Cavendish, "An Epistle to the Reader," *The Worlds Olio*, n. p. I have silently modernized the spelling and punctuation.

[51] Although she describes her fruitless efforts to secure some kind of provision from parliament at length in her autobiography, Cavendish refers to her writing only briefly, noting that "part" of her time in England was spent in writing "a book of poems and a little book called my *Philosophical Fancies*." Cavendish, *True Relation*, in Firth, ed., *Life of William Cavendish*, 170. I have silently modernized the spelling and punctuation.

[52] On the hectic pace of Cavendish's writing, see Whitaker, *Mad Madge*, 157-58. Interestingly, while *Poems, and Fancies* appeared in the folio format she favored, the

Early in 1653, after eighteen months in England, Cavendish finally received a warrant allowing her to leave country and return to her husband in Antwerp—and to the work she had put aside and locked in a trunk. But, having given the material "a resurrection," she realized that it was not quite what she remembered. She looked over what she had written and "judged it not so well done," but Cavendish decided to publish her work anyway: "I, being of a lazy disposition, did choose to let it go into the world with its defects rather than take the pains to refine it."[53] With the same kind of defensiveness she would later show when she published her collections of plays, Cavendish acknowledges what her critics might say even while she claims not to care. "I am so well armed with carelessness that their several censures can never enter to vex me with wounds of discontent," she writes; "I have my delight in writing and having it printed, and if any take a delight to read it, I will not thank them for it, for if anything please therein, they are to thank me for so much pleasure, and if it be naught, I had rather they had left it unread."[54]

She titled her collection *The World's Olio*, named after a Spanish stew, *olla podrida*, a highly spiced and rich mixture of meats and vegetables.[55] In a preface to this spicy mix, Cavendish raised the issue of the obvious disparity between the education women receive and that offered to men. She begins by acknowledging her deficiencies, explaining that she cannot be expected to write "so wisely or so wittily as men" because she is of "the effeminate sex." She then sets out to "give reason" why, as a

---

second publication—written in just three weeks (Whitaker, *Mad Madge*, 157)—was published in a small, octavo format.

For an introduction to Cavendish's philosophical ideas, see *The Stanford Encyclopedia of Philosophy* [online], Winter 2016, s.v. "Margaret Lucas Cavendish," by David Cunning, http://plato.stanford.edu/entries/margaret-cavendish/.

For a detailed chronology of Cavendish's published work, see Appendix, 165-68.

[53] Cavendish, "An Epistle to the Reader," *The Worlds Olio*, n. p. I have silently modernized the spelling and punctuation. On her comments about her problems with grammar and spelling, see "A Note on the Text," below, 102-5.

[54] Cavendish, "An Epistle to the Reader," *The Worlds Olio*, n. p. I have silently modernized the spelling and punctuation.

[55] "A spiced meat and vegetable stew of Spanish and Portuguese origin. Hence: any dish containing a great variety of ingredients" (*Oxford English Dictionary* [online], www.oed.com, hereafter cited as *OED*). The *OED* also records Cavendish's use of the word here as the first example of "olio" in this figurative sense: "A collection of various artistic or literary pieces, a book containing miscellaneous items (such as engravings, or poems) on various subjects."

woman, she "cannot be so wise as men," although first she begs "pardon" of her readers, female and male alike. She predicts that women will condemn her "out of partiality to themselves" and that men will condemn her either because they wish to curry favor with women or, for their own "comfort and ease," because they know that "women's tongues are like stings of bees." No man would knowingly rile up a "monarchy" of female bees to "swarm around [his] ears" and sting him to death.[56]

But the self-deprecation of Cavendish's opening apology quickly gives way to the kind of anger that, in Woolf's view, "disfigured" her work. Cavendish argues that men and women were "made equal by nature," but that men had, "from their first creation, usurped a superiority to themselves" and then had unjustly maintained this "tyrannical government" ever since. Women "could never come to be free" and thus grew more and more "enslaved," treated by men "like children, fools, or subjects." Her conclusions about women's "slavery" are chilling: "we are become so stupid that beasts are but a degree below us, and men use us but a degree above beasts." Cavendish holds out a brief hope for women's education—"if we were bred in schools to mature our brains and to manure our understandings, . . . we might bring forth the fruits of knowledge." But at this point, almost as if she fears where her argument is leading her, Cavendish backs away. Although she refutes Adam's superiority to Eve in one of the essays printed *inside* the spicy stew of *The World's Olio*, the rest of her prefatory letter to her readers is an extended analysis not of men and women's equality but of men's superiority—they are stronger and their brains are better, "more clear to understand and to contrive than women's." Aside from giving birth, men perform virtually every useful function to society, from tilling fields to governing states.[57]

Her acceptance of male superiority leads Cavendish to conclude that women are properly ruled by men. Even so, she is a strong advocate for women's education. Just as barren ground, properly tilled and amply "manured" will produce "plentiful crops" and "diverse sorts of flowers," women's minds, enlarged by education, "may come to be far more

---

[56] Cavendish, "Preface to the Reader," *The Worlds Olio*, n. p. I have silently modernized the spelling and punctuation.

[57] Cavendish, "Preface to the Reader," *The Worlds Olio*, n. p. I have silently modernized the spelling and punctuation.

knowing and learned." Cavendish doesn't offer women's intellectual inferiority and their proper subordination to men as an excuse for their ignorance, however. In Cavendish's words, "being subject" to men is "no hindrance from thinking." Sounding much like Virginia Woolf some three centuries later, Cavendish insists that "thoughts are free." Whatever women's physical circumstances, their minds "can never be enslaved."[58] Thus women are "not hindered from studying." Men may have their colleges and universities, but women, or at least women of a certain class, have their "closets" where they are free to read and to study.

Cavendish also wrote about the state of female education in a letter she addresses to the "famously learned" men of Oxford and Cambridge, included as a preface to her *Philosophical and Physical Opinions*, published in the same year as *The World's Olio*. In this letter, Cavendish expresses her fear that women "grow irrational as idiots" because of the "careless neglects and despisements of the masculine sex to the female, thinking it impossible [women] should have either learning or understanding, wit or judgment, as if [they] had not rational souls as well as men." And because such attitudes are customary, Cavendish fears that women, out of their "dejectedness," will come to "think so too" and be content occupying themselves with "low and petty employments." Without the encouragement to exercise their "higher capacities," women "are become like worms, that only live in the dull earth of ignorance, winding ourselves sometimes out by the help of some refreshing rain of good education, which seldom is given us, for we are kept like birds in cages, to hop up and down in our houses, not suffered to fly abroad." Women lack variety—"changes of fortune"—and experience; they lack "understanding and knowledge, and so, consequently, prudence." Thus deprived, they "are shut out of all power and authority": "we are never employed either in civil or martial affairs, our counsels are despised and laughed at," she writes, "the best of our actions are trodden down with scorn, by the overweening conceit men have of themselves and through a despisement of us."[59]

---

[58] As Woolf wrote, "Lock up your libraries if you like; but there is no gate, no lock, no bolt that you can set upon the freedom of my mind." Woolf, *A Room of One's Own*, 76.

[59] Margaret Cavendish, "To the Two Universities," *Philosophical and Physical Opinions* (1655), n. p. I have silently modernized the spelling and punctuation.

Cavendish's next work, *Nature's Pictures*, is a collection of "poetical" and "romancical" stories, told both in verse and in prose. Her goal in these narratives is not simply to amuse but to instruct; as she describes the "design" of her "feigned stories," the aim is "to present virtue" to her readers, "the muses leading her, and the graces attending on her, to defend innocence, help the distressed, lament the unfortunate, and show that vice is seldom crowned with good success." Here, too, she informs her reader about the drive that fuels her as a *writer* even as she acknowledges the constraints upon her as a *woman*: "That my ambition of extraordinary fame is restless and not ordinary I cannot deny, and since all heroic actions, public employments, as well civil as military, and eloquent pleadings are denied my sex in this age, I may be excused for writing so much, for that is the reason I have run, more busily than industriously, upon every subject I can think of."[60] The whole is conceived of as a frame-tale narrative, not unlike Chaucer's *Canterbury Tales*, with a small group of men and women deciding to entertain themselves by telling stories:

In winter cold a company was met,
Both men and women by the fire were set;
At last they did agree to pass the time
That everyone should tell a tale in rhyme;
The women said, "We no true measures know,
Nor do our rhymes in even numbers go";
"Why," said the men, "All women's tongues are free
To speak both out of time and foolishly,"
And, drawing lots, the chance fell on a man,
Who having spit and blown his nose, began.[61]

---

[60] Cavendish, "The Preface," *Natures Pictures*, n. p. I have silently modernized the spelling and punctuation.

[61] Cavendish, *Natures Pictures*, [2]. I have silently modernized the spelling and punctuation. Cavendish's use of the frame-tale narrative is interesting, since, in addition to Chaucer's use of the format in *The Canterbury Tales*, it is also a genre used by women writers. Cavendish herself may have known about Christine de Pizan's *Book of the City of Ladies*, composed in 1405; Cristina Malcolmson has argued that the Cavendishes acquired a lavishly illustrated manuscript collection of Pizan's work while they were in exile on the continent. Malcolmson, "Christine de Pizan's *City of Ladies* in Early Modern England," in *Debating Gender in Early Modern Europe, 1500-1700*, ed. Cristina Malcolmson and Mihoko Suzuki, Early Modern Cultural Studies (Palgrave Macmillan, 2002), 15-36.

The "feigned stories" in verse that follow in the first book include several Cavendish calls "mock tales" that are recounted by her husband. As she turns from verse narratives to prose—at which point she also abandons the framing narrative that had unified her first group of stories—she continues to include stories she attributes to her husband, notably one delightful piece titled "His Grace the Duke of Newcastle's Opinion, 'Whether a Cat Seeth in the Night, or No?'"[62] There are also several longer prose narratives in *Nature's Pictures*, in particular three that we might regard as *novellas*, "The Contract," "Assaulted and Pursued Chastity," and "The She Anchoret."[63] The volume concludes with her autobiography, *A True Relation of My Birth, Breeding, and Life*. As Cavendish's biographer Katie Whitaker notes, this collection was "exceptional": "Mary Wroth was the only woman to have published a work of original English fiction before Margaret, with disastrous results, and no woman had ever published—or probably even written—an autobiography like Margaret's."[64]

By this point, Margaret had also begun writing plays. She would later claim that her decision to write drama was inspired by her husband— during their exile on the continent, he was writing plays and reading them aloud to her, carefully putting them aside, waiting "for a good time" when they might be performed. While her husband could afford to withhold his efforts from publication in the hope that English theaters might at some point be reopened and his plays staged, Margaret Cavendish knew that she could not keep her own plays "concealed in the hopes to have them first acted."[65] No woman had ever seen her play acted on a public stage in England. The publication of her collection of plays was, however, delayed by political events. In 1658, Oliver

---

The frame-tale format was also used by Marguerite de Navarre (1492-1549), sister of Francis I of France, in her *Heptameron*, published posthumously in 1559, and by the Spanish writer Maria de Zayas y Sotomayor (1590-1661), who published two frame-tale narratives, *Amorous and Exemplary Novels*, in 1637, and *The Disenchantments of Love*, in 1647.

[62] Cavendish, *Natures Pictures*, 568-70.

[63] "The Contract" and "Assaulted and Pursued Chastity" are included in Margaret Cavendish, *The Blazing World and Other Writings*, ed. Kate Lilley (New York: Penguin Books, 1994), 1-118.

[64] Whitaker, *Mad Madge*, 197. For reactions to Wroth's publication, see above, n. 42.

[65] "The Epistle Dedicatory," *Playes* (London, 1662), A3r. I have silently modernized the spelling and punctuation.

Cromwell, Lord Protector of England during the Commonwealth period, died. He was succeeded briefly and unsuccessfully by his son, Richard, but after seven months, the younger Cromwell was removed from office, and on 8 May 1660, Parliament decided that Charles II had been king since his father was executed in 1649. The Stuart monarch was recalled from exile and returned to England in May 1660. After sixteen long years, Margaret and William Cavendish were also able to return to England.

Although William Cavendish would ultimately be rewarded for his loyalty with the title of duke of Newcastle, he did not receive the kind of political appointment he had hoped for, nor was it a simple matter for him to recover his lost property.[66] By September, the Cavendishes left London for Welbeck Abbey, William's estate near Nottingham.[67] The couple would spend the majority of their time together there in quiet retirement, devoting themselves to reading and writing. As Virginia Woolf would later describe their lives, with not a little degree of acerbity, "they lived together in the depths of the country in the greatest seclusion and perfect contentment, scribbling plays, poems, philosophies, greeting each other's works with raptures of delight, and confabulating, doubtless, upon such marvels of the natural world as chance threw their way."[68] In splendid isolation and with her husband's devoted support, Margaret Cavendish could continue to write. And with some restoration of their finances, she could also employ a secretary to prepare her work for publication and to oversee proof copies. She could also dispense with booksellers, whom she had blamed for many of the problems with her earlier publications, instead choosing her own printers and financing her projects herself. As Katie Whitaker notes, this "arrangement gave her

---

[66] William Cavendish received the title of "duke" in 1665. Margaret details carefully and at length all of the material losses her husband had suffered during the civil wars; on his "confused, entangled, and almost ruined estate," see Cavendish, *The Life of . . . William Cavendishe . . .* , in Firth, ed., *Life of William Cavendish*, 68-81.

[67] After the dissolution of the monasteries, begun by Thomas Cromwell during the reign of Henry VIII, the abbey was purchased by Richard Whalley in 1539; after Whalley's death in November 1583, Welbeck was purchased by Gilbert Talbot, earl of Shrewsbury. Talbot had been married to Elizabeth Cavendish, the daughter of Bess of Hardwick, in 1568, at the same time his father, George Talbot, married Bess (it was her fourth marriage). In 1607, Welbeck was sold to Bess of Hardwick's son, Charles Cavendish, William Cavendish's father. William Cavendish inherited Welbeck in 1617.

[68] Woolf, *The Common Reader*, 72.

much greater control over production and resulted in more careful printing, without the numerous errors of her earlier works."[69]

Her first publication after the Restoration was *Plays*, which appeared early in 1662. Later in the year, in the fall, experimenting with yet another genre, she published *Orations of Divers Sorts*.[70] Cavendish also began to devote herself to the study of science; while in Antwerp, she had met the Dutch poet and diplomat Constantijn Huygens, who was himself very interested in the new science, and she had made him a present of her *Poems and Fancies* when it was published in 1653. (Unlike Hobbes and Descartes, he may have spoken *to* her, but he also spoke *about* her, writing to a correspondent—one of her husband's distant cousins—that he had received Cavendish's "wonderful book," but that reading about her "extravagant atoms kept me from sleeping a great part of last night in this my little solitude."[71]) The two had begun a correspondence about

---

[69] Whitaker, *Mad Madge*, 244.

[70] Margaret Cavendish, *Orations of Divers Sorts, Accommodated to Divers Places* (London, 1662). In a series of seven "Female Orations" included in the collection (225-32), the individual speakers lay out a range of varying positions on the topic of women's equality to men, their freedom, and their potential.

[71] Constantijn Huygens to Utricia Ogle Swann, 15 September 1653, in J. A. Worp, ed., *Die Briefwisseling van Constantijn Huygens, 1608-1687*, vol. 5, *1649-1663* (The Hague: Martinus Nijhoff, 1916), 186-87. Utricia Ogle Swann was a member of the court of Mary Henrietta Stuart, Charles I and Henrietta Maria's daughter, who had married William, prince of Orange. (Ogle was related to William Cavendish through his mother, Catherine Ogle). Constantijn Huygens (1596-1687) was a diplomat and had been knighted by James I of England in 1622, later filling a number of official roles for the princes of Orange. He was also the father of the noted Dutch mathematician and scientist Christiaan Huygens.

It is hard to gauge the tone of his comment about Cavendish and her "extravagant atoms," but it is clearly different from the one he adopted in his letters to Margaret Cavendish herself, two of which are included in William Cavendish's *Letters and Poems in Honour of the Incomparable Princess, Margaret, Dutchess of Newcastle* (London, 1676). In the first of these, dated 12 March 1657, Huygens expresses his gratitude for an afternoon's conversation and promises he will return soon to her "school" where she will "once again be bountiful" to his "ignorance" (119-20); in the second, dated 28 November 1658, he records having presented a collection of her published work to the University of Leyden, as she had requested (1-2).

Several other letters from Huygens to Margaret Cavendish are in Worp's edition: from 20 March 1657, 27 March 1657, 30 March 1657, 12 October 1658, 11 January 1659 (all in vol. 5); from 12 August 1664 and 19 September 1671, in vol. 6, *1663-1687* (The Hague: Martinus Nijhoff, 1917). A facsimile of this multi-volume edition is reprinted, in its entirety, as *Correspondence of Constantijn Huygens 1608-1687* (Huygens Institute for the History of the Netherlands in The Hague, 2010), available online at

science, one allowing Cavendish to express her scientific theories and even to attempt some scientific experiments, but as her biographer Douglas Grant observes, Cavendish's letters to Huygens demonstrate "the principal difficulties which hindered her as a natural philosopher": first, her lack of education, which she attempted to remedy, and second, the overwhelming opposition to women "dabbling" in science, which it was impossible for her to overcome. Grant concludes that "the few experiments she might conduct in Huygens's sympathetic company were a poor substitute" for formal training and careful experimentation.[72] Still, Cavendish carried on her correspondence with Huygens, and if it did not lead to Cavendish herself becoming a key figure in the Scientific Revolution, it did result in her revision of earlier work. Dissatisfied with her *Philosophical and Physical Opinions*, originally published in 1655, she revised and expanded it, publishing a second edition in 1663. She also found a way into the discourse of philosophy and science in her *Philosophical Letters, or Modest Reflections upon Some Opinions in Natural Philosophy Maintained by Several Famous and Learned Authors of This Age, Expressed by Way of Letters*.[73]

The Cavendishes did leave Welbeck and travel to London on occasion, in 1665, for example, after William Cavendish received the title duke of Newcastle, and again in 1667. They attended court during their 1665 stay in London, and although they were still in debt and their finances shaky, they spent lavishly. This visit was brief, however. In 1666, while she was back in Welbeck, Cavendish's *Observations upon Experimental Philosophy, to Which is Added "The Description of a New Blazing World"* was published, the first of a series of works printed by her new printer, Anne Maxwell. By the time the Cavendishes returned to London in 1667, William Cavendish had at last recovered his town residence, Newcastle House, built in Clerkenwell Close on the grounds of a former nunnery.[74]

---

http://resources.huygens.knaw.nl/briefwisselingconstantijnhuygens/en. The website also makes available facsimile copies of most of the letters.

[72] Grant, *Margaret the First*, 195-96.

[73] See above, 16.

[74] The property had formerly belonged to St. Mary's nunnery, suppressed in 1539. It was a fashionable neighborhood in the seventeenth century. After William Cavendish had acquired the property in the 1630s, the large mansion was renamed Newcastle House, and he spent considerable money in building and renovating. During his years in exile, the trustees for his sequestered property had sold it. On his return to England, it took William Cavendish several years, a court case, and the sale of some of his other

There they entertained widely, and the king himself paid them the compliment of a visit.

During their stay in London, the famously shy Margaret Cavendish became the talk of the city. For one thing, she was given to "masculine" conversation—that is, she was known to speak openly, confidently, and authoritatively on such topics as poetry, science, philosophy, and theology. And then there was her manner of dress. In her autobiography, she had described her youthful love of clothing, especially the pieces she "invented" for herself, taking "delight" in the "singularity" of her creations; now her "singular" costumes attracted a great deal of attention. In her public appearances, she sometimes affected male attire, or, rather, a hybrid mixture of male and female apparel, a fact noted by one observer who commented on her meeting with the duke of York. The somewhat bemused writer reported that Margaret's "behavior was very pleasant, but rather to be seen than told." She "was dressed in a vest," an item of masculine clothing, and rather than making an appropriate curtsey, she "made legs and bows to the ground with her hand at her head."[75]

The diarist Samuel Pepys tried repeatedly to see the duchess in London, his first efforts proving fruitless because of the crowds that gathered whenever and wherever she was rumored to make an appearance. When he finally did manage to get a glimpse of Cavendish, she was wearing a knee-length outer coat and a velvet cap, both garments inspired by fashionable male attire (the cap was a type favored by Christina of Sweden, also known for wearing male clothing).[76] Her costumes attracted attention for other reasons as well. When she attended a public performance of a play written by her husband, one member of the audience reported that she herself "was all the pageant

---

property in order to regain the house. On this see *Survey of London*, vol. 66: *South and East Clerkenwell*, ed. Phillip Temple (London: London County Council, 2008), 28-39, http://www.british-history.ac.uk/survey-london/ vol46 /pp28-39.

[75] Sir Charles Lyttelton (of Hagley Hall) to his cousin Sir Christopher Lyttleton (later viscount of Hatton), 7 August 1665. In *Correspondence of the Family of Hatton . . . 1607-1704*, ed. Edward M. Thompson, Camden Society n. s., vol. 22 (London: Camden Society, 1878), 1:47. I have silently modernized the spelling and punctuation.

[76] Samuel Pepys, 26 April 1667, in *The Diary of Samuel Pepys . . .* , ed. Henry B. Wheatley (New York: Macmillan, 1895), 6:290. Pepys made repeated efforts to see Cavendish during her visit to London, recording his various attempts on 11 April, 1 May, and 10 May.

now discoursed on"; she was wearing "an antic dress" cut so low that her breasts were "all laid out to view," her nipples "scarlet trimmed."[77] But at least one contemporary seemed to enjoy Cavendish's appearance rather than pretending to be scandalized by it. On 18 April, Sir John Evelyn, who had known the couple since their exile in Paris, visited Newcastle House; he was received there "with great kindness," he writes, adding that he was "much pleased with the extraordinary fanciful habit, garb, and discourse of the duchess." He visited her at home again on 25 April and on 27 April with his wife, whom Cavendish "received with a kind of transport, suitable to her extravagant humor and dress, which was very singular."[78] Mary Evelyn was less impressed than her husband. While she thought Cavendish's "habit" was "particular, fantastical, not unbecoming a good shape," she thought her conversation was as "airy, empty, whimsical, and rambling as her books, aiming at science, difficulties, high notions, terminating commonly in nonsense, oaths, and obscenity." She judged Cavendish to be "more than necessarily submissive," and while the duchess might affect humility, Mary Evelyn

---

[77] Sir Charles North to his father, 13 April 1667, quoted in Susan Wiseman, *Drama and Politics in the English Civil War* (New York, Cambridge University Press, 1998), 93. I have silently modernized the spelling and punctuation. Some of Cavendish's modern critics assume that the word "antic," should be understood as "antique," thus referring to a dress in the classical style, but Sophie Tomlinson notes that "antic" in this context more likely refers to the costume's strangeness. Tomlinson, *Women on Stage in Stuart Drama* (New York: Cambridge University Press, 2005), 183. The *OED* records several contemporary uses of the adjective "antic" to describe "dress or attire": "Absurd from fantastic incongruity; grotesque, bizarre, uncouthly ludicrous" (*OED*).

The play Margaret Cavendish was attending was her husband's *The Humorous Lovers*. Pepys attended a performance of this play on 11 April 1667, although he believed the play was by Margaret Cavendish rather than her husband. Pepys thought the play was "the most ridiculous thing that ever was wrote" (*The Diary of Samuel Pepys*, ed. Wheatley, 6:269). His opinion might perhaps have been different had he known the play was by William Cavendish rather than his wife—but, then again, maybe not (see below, n. 139).

Pepys was not the only person to believe that *The Humorous Lovers* was by Margaret, and not William, Cavendish—her authorship was also assumed by Gervaise Jaquis, who in May 1667 noted that, "upon Monday last, the duchess of Newcastle's play was acted in the theater in Lincoln's Inn Field, the king and the grandees of the court being present, and so was her grace and the duke, her husband." Gervaise Jaquis to the earl of Huntington, May 1667, quoted in Nancy Cotton, *Women Playwrights in England, c. 1363-1750* (Lewisburg, PA: Bucknell University Press, 1980), 48-49.

[78] John Evelyn, 27 April 1667, in *The Diary of John Evelyn*, ed. William Bray (London: George Bell, 1889), 2:25-26. I have silently modernized the spelling and punctuation.

concludes, "Never did I see a woman so full of herself, so amazingly vain and ambitious."[79]

In yet another example of what Sophie Tomlinson has identified as Cavendish's "rhetoric of dress and behavior," Cavendish was honored by an invitation to the newly established Royal Society in London.[80] On 30 May 1667 she became the first woman to attend a meeting of the society (which didn't admit women as members until 1945). Pepys was present on the occasion of her visit, although he implies that he showed up at Arundel House not realizing that the Society's regular Tuesday meeting had been altered to Thursday—it had apparently taken some time for members to decide whether Cavendish would be invited. Pepys notes that there had been "much debate, pro and con," adding, "it seems many being against it."[81] Cavendish made an impressive entrance, arriving "with her women attending her" and waited on by an eager "company" gathered in expectation of her arrival. Once there, she was treated to a series of scientific experiments, including a demonstration of Robert Boyle's air pump and of Robert Hooke's microscope. Cavendish had once imagined such an occasion, where she was the only woman honored among a group of illustrious men. In her fictional version of such a meeting, she described herself as "extremely out of countenance," not sure "how to behave," and full of "bashfulness"; overwhelmed by the experience, she "made the more haste to depart."[82] The real experience was much the same as her imagined version; as Pepys tells the story, after the various demonstrations, she "cried still she was full of admiration" and then promptly left. "I do not like her at all," he concludes, "nor did I hear her say anything that was worth hearing, but that she was full of admiration, all admiration."[83] In his account of events, Evelyn is more circumspect, noting in his diary that Cavendish arrived "in great pomp" and that he "conducted her to her coach" when

---

[79] Mary Evelyn to the Rev. Ralph Bohun, undated letter from 1667, in *The Diary and Correspondence of John Evelyn*, ed. William Bray (London: Henry Colburn, 1857), 4:8-9. I have silently modernized the spelling and punctuation.

[80] Tomlinson, *Women on Stage*, 183.

[81] Pepys, 30 May 1667, in *Diary of Samuel Pepys*, ed. Wheatley, 6:343. I have silently modernized the spelling and punctuation

[82] Cavendish, Letter 199, *Sociable Letters*, 417-19. I have silently modernized the spelling and punctuation.

[83] Pepys, 30 May 1667, in *Diary of Samuel Pepys*, ed. Wheatley, 6:344. I have silently modernized the spelling and punctuation.

the experiments were over.[84] But if he is indeed the author of the light-hearted verses attributed to him, composed on the occasion of her visit to the Royal Society, he may have shared his wife's rather less charitable view of the duchess and her ambitions:

> But . . . her head gear was so pretty
> I ne'er saw anything so witty
> Though I was half afeared
> God bless us! When I first did see her
> She looked so like a cavalier
> But that she had no beard![85]

Just days after Cavendish's attendance at the meeting with the Royal Society, London was in turmoil. In early June, the Dutch fleet sailed up the Thames and burned several war ships. The frightening event was reported by both Pepys and Evelyn—perhaps as fearful of English looters as the Dutch invaders. Pepys made his will and sent his wife, father, and money into the country, while Evelyn commented on the widespread panic that sent everyone "flying, none knew why or whither," and busied himself surveying the damage and lamenting the "dishonor."[86] Margaret Cavendish and her husband, meanwhile, remained in London. They did not leave until after the crisis had passed and the Dutch were gone, quietly leaving for Welbeck in July. Their departure was unremarked by all of those who had paid such attention to them earlier.

Back in Welbeck, Margaret Cavendish resumed her fevered program of writing and publication. In the summer of 1667 she published her biography of her husband, *The Life of the Thrice Noble, High, Puissant Prince William Cavendish, Duke, Marquess, and Earl of Newcastle*, and then, in 1668, *Plays, Never before Printed*. She also published new editions of previously

---

[84] John Evelyn, 30 May 1667, in *Diary of John Evelyn*, ed. Bray, 2:26. I have silently modernized the spelling and punctuation.

[85] Quoted in Jones, *A Glorious Fame*, 163. Jones indicates that the anonymous "scurrilous verses" were attributed to Evelyn.

[86] Pepys, in *Diary of Samuel Pepys*, ed. Wheatley, 6:354-71, and Evelyn, in *Diary of John Evelyn*, ed. Bray, 2:26-30. I have silently modernized the spelling and punctuation. The so-called raid on the Medway was part of the second Anglo-Dutch War and occurred between 19 and 24 June 1667 (though Pepys and Evelyn both date their diary entries between 9 and 14 June in the Old Style).

published work: a Latin translation by Walter Charleton of her biography of her husband; the *Grounds of Natural Philosophy*, a reissued, "much altered," version of *Philosophical and Physical Opinions*; a second edition of *Observations upon Experimental Philosophy, to Which is Added "The Description of a New Blazing World"*; a separate publication of *The Description of a New World, Called the Blazing-World*; *Poems, or Several Fancies in Verse, with the Animal Parliament, in Prose*; a third edition of *Poems and Fancies*; and a second edition of *Orations of Divers Sorts, Accommodated to Divers Places*. But then the hectic pace slowed. Two earlier works were reissued in 1671, *Nature's Pictures* and *The World's Olio*, both in second editions. But there was nothing new.

Constantijn Huygens visited London that fall, and although he wrote to Cavendish in September, he did not make the trip to Welbeck to see her. In July of 1672, she received a package of books and pens from Mark Anthony Benoist, who had been a tutor to William Cavendish's sons. This was followed, a month later, by a letter from him, a reply to one of hers. She had sent him some "filings" of a lodestone along with the result of some experiments she had conducted. He assured her he would show her letter to "several persons, to have their opinions whether it be right or no."[87] But a year later, in June of 1673, she still had not reimbursed Benoist for the items he had sent. And then, on 15 December 1673, she suddenly died at Welbeck Abbey. She was fifty years old.

On 3 January 1674, her body left Welbeck for London. She lay in state for several days at Newcastle House before her burial in Westminster Abbey. As a tribute to his wife, her husband published the *Letters and Poems in Honor of the Incomparable Princess, Margaret, Duchess of Newcastle* in 1676.

Margaret Cavendish's literary career began in 1653, with the publication of her first poems and "philosophical fancies," and continued at a hectic pace for nearly two decades. She did not limit herself to genres "acceptable" for those few women who did publish in the early seventeenth century, lyric poems, devotional works, and personal letters, for example. Instead, she published two volumes of plays, philosophical and scientific works, a utopian romance that has often been called the

---

[87] Quoted in Whitaker, *Mad Madge*, 236.

first work of science fiction in English, a biography of her husband, and her own autobiography, *A True Relation of My Birth, Breeding, and Life*.

It can be hard to assess the significance of her publication today, but as her recent biographer, Katie Whitaker, reminds us, "In the first forty years of the [seventeenth] century fewer than eighty books by women had been published in England—making up only one-half of 1 percent of all books—and many of these had appeared only posthumously, or else in pirated editions, without their authors' consent."[88] But for two short decades, Margaret Cavendish wrote and published as if she were trying to make up the difference all by herself.

Women, Performance, and Playwriting in Early-Modern England

When the young Margaret Lucas she attended the theater with her sisters, she would not have seen women players on the stage. Women did not perform in the comedies and tragedies produced at the great London playhouses like Blackfriars, the Boar's Head, the Fortune, the Phoenix, and the Red Bull. Outside of the commercial playhouses, however, there was a history of female performance in England—from the Benedictine nuns of Barking Abbey, who played the roles of the three Marys in a series of Holy Week and Easter plays in the fourteenth century, to Moll Frith's infamous appearance at the Fortune in 1611, when she "sat upon the stage in the public view of all the people there present in man's apparel and played upon her lute and sang a song" and "spoke immodest and lascivious speeches."[89] Women in towns and cities across England took part in civic pageants devised to honor visiting dignitaries, danced in parishes to raise money for charitable purposes,

---

[88] Whitaker, *Mad Madge*, xiii.

[89] On the nuns of Barking, see Laurie A. Finke, *Women's Writing in English: Medieval England*, Women's Writing in English (New York: Longman, 1999), 110-11, and Katie Normington, *Gender and Medieval Drama*, Gender in the Middle Ages (Cambridge, UK: D. S. Brewer, 2004), 48-49. For more on the nuns at Barking Abbey, see below, 39).

The performance of Moll—or Mary—Frith has received considerable attention, but I recommend the account in Stephen Orgel's *Impersonations: The Performance of Gender in Shakespeare's England* (New York: Cambridge University Press, 1996), 139-53. The Consistory Court of London's Correction Book, with its account of Moll's subsequent appearance before the ecclesiastical court, is in S. P. Cerasano and Marion Wynne-Davies, eds., *Renaissance Drama by Women: Texts and Documents* (New York: Routledge, 1996), 172 (I have silently modernized the spelling and punctuation).

entertained guests in private houses, played the role of the May queen at May Day festivals, and, at least on occasion, performed in the communal and collaborative mystery plays that were popular well into the sixteenth century.[90] Itinerant troupes of performers—singers, acrobats, tumblers, and jugglers—played on makeshift stages on the street, in town squares and courtyards, at inns and ale houses, anywhere they could draw an audience. And aristocratic women regularly took part in court performances and masques—Anne Boleyn's first documented appearance at the Tudor court of Henry VIII was on 1 March 1522, when she participated in the *Chateau Vert* pageant in the role of Perseverance (her sister Mary was Kindness)—while Elizabeth Tudor's entire queenship has been described by many modern historians as an extended and consummate public performance.[91] The queen herself seemed to make that very point in her 1586 speech to parliament: "Princes, you know, stand upon stages so that their actions are viewed and beheld of all men."[92]

At the court of James I, Elizabeth's successor, Queen Anna of Denmark and her ladies performed in masques, including Samuel Daniel's *The Vision of the Twelve Goddesses*, on 8 January 1604, in which the queen took the role of Pallas Athena, and Ben Jonson's *The Masque of*

---

[90] See Normington, *Gender and Medieval Drama*, 48-52. Whether women performed in medieval drama is a vexed question, but Normington documents the performance of some "wyffs" (wives) of Chester in 1499 and 1539-40, and, while noting the ambiguity of this reference, points out the unambiguous participation of women in the Innocents play of Coventry, where they "sang before the slaughter of their children by Herod's soldiers" (40-41).

[91] For Anne Boleyn, see Eric Ives, *Anne Boleyn* (Cambridge, MA: Blackwell, 1988), 47. The literature on Queen Elizabeth's self-representation is large; see, for a start, Susan Frye, *Elizabeth I: The Competition for Representation* (New York: Oxford University Press, 1993); Carole Levin, *The Heart and Stomach of a King: Elizabeth I and the Politics of Sex and Power* (Philadelphia: University of Pennsylvania Press, 1994); and Helen Hackett, *Virgin Mother, Maiden Queen: Elizabeth I and the Cult of the Virgin Mary* (New York: St. Martin's Press, 1995).

[92] Queen Elizabeth's First Reply to Parliament, 12 November 1586, in *Elizabeth I: Collected Works*, ed. Leah S. Marcus, Janel Mueller, and Mary Beth Rose (Chicago: University of Chicago Press, 2000), 189. This version of the queen's speech represents "a contemporary report of the speech, and probably close to the speech as the queen delivered it to the parliamentary delegates who waited on her with their petition at Richmond. Since she spoke impromptu, all MSS were created after the fact" (186n1). A second copy, this one published, phrases the metaphor somewhat differently: "for we princes, I tell you, are set on stages in the sight and view of all the world duly observed" (194).

Blackness, on 6 January 1605, with the queen as Euphoris, one of the twelve daughters of Niger, and Lady Mary Wroth—whose publication of *Urania* in 1621 drew such negative attention—as another, Baryte. The queen also appeared in Jonson's companion piece to *Blackness*, *The Masque of Beauty*, performed in on 10 January 1608, this time with sixteen women of the court participating. As queen, Anna performed in twelve court masques, including Daniel's *Tethys' Festival*, in 1610, which celebrated her son Henry's investiture as prince of Wales, but she stopped performing after Prince Henry's untimely death in 1612. These courtly performances were not without criticism; the Privy Council expressed reservations about the appropriateness of the queen's performance as well as concern about the expense of the productions.[93] For his part, the courtier Dudley Carleton disapproved of the queen's costume, if not the performance itself—in his comments on the queen's appearance as Pallas Athena, Carleton complained that the queen's dress was too short, revealing her feet and legs—and he criticized the women's costumes in *The Masque of Blackness* as well—they were "too light and courtesan-like for such great ones."[94] It's important to note, however, that while royal and aristocratic women participated in Jacobean court masques, the female performers were silent: they danced, but they did not speak.

One noteworthy example of women's performance not *by* the queen but *for* her occurred in 1617, when the "young gentlewomen of the Ladies Hall in Deptford" performed Robert White's *Cupid's Banishment*.[95] These "young gentlewomen" were not part of the Stuart court, nor were they performing at Whitehall, but neither did they lack court connections; two of the queen's goddaughters attended the school, and

---

[93] The Council to James I, December 1604, with its concern about the appropriateness of the queen's performance, is quoted in Tomlinson, *Women on Stage*, 2. On the Privy Council's concerns about the expense of the masques, see, for example, Leeds Barroll, "Inventing the Stuart Masque," in *The Politics of the Stuart Court Masque*, ed. David Bevington and Peter Holbrooke (New York: Cambridge University Press, 2006), 132.

[94] Dudley Carleton's criticism of Queen Anne's costume is quoted in Cerasano and Wynne-Davies, eds., *Renaissance Drama by Women*, 80; Carleton's criticism of the costumes in *The Masque of Blackness* is quoted in Tomlinson, *Women on Stage*, 25. I have silently modernized the spelling and punctuation.

[95] Robert White was the master of Ladies Hall, which Cerasano and Wynne-Davies describe as "a school located south of London in Deptford. . . . It seems to have been a sort of high-class private academy that offered both academic studies and training in social skills." Cerasano and Wynne-Davies, eds., *Renaissance Drama by Women*, 77.

the masque was dedicated to Lucy Russell, the countess of Bedford, who had regularly performed in court masques with the queen, including *The Vision of the Twelve Goddesses*, *The Masque of Blackness*, and *The Masque of Beauty*. But, while *Cupid's Banishment* may not have been performed at the king's court, it was performed at the *queen's* court, Greenwich Palace—and, most importantly, a young woman playing the role of Fortune spoke during the performance. In her analysis of this masque, Clare McManus claims that *Cupid's Banishment* is "a document of immense importance for the assessment of female performance" in early-modern England: though the masque itself was "insubstantial" and "derivative," it marks the moment when "the female masquing voice was first heard."[96]

Anna of Denmark's daughter-in-law, Henrietta Maria of France, not only continued the masquing tradition but was also a patron of and performer in pastoral dramas presented at the Caroline court. In December of 1625, just months after her marriage to King Charles I, the queen began rehearsing her "troupe" for a performance of *Artenice*, a comedy based on Honorat de Bueil, sieur de Racan's *Les Bergeries* ("the sheepfold"). In February 1626, when Henrietta Maria played the lead role of Artenice, she shocked the audience by performing a speaking role. The audience was also surprised by the spectacle of women playing the parts of men.[97] The Venetian ambassador to London appreciated the "rich scenery and dresses" of the queen and "her maidens," as well as the queen's "remarkable acting," but, as he also observed, "it did not give complete satisfaction because the English objected to the first part being declaimed by the queen." Another observer commented, "I have known the time when this would have seemed a strange sight, to see a queen act

---

[96] Clare McManus, *Women on the Renaissance Stage: Anna of Denmark and Female Masquing in the Stuart Court, 1590-1619* (Manchester, UK: Manchester University Press, 2002), 164-201. McManus's comment on the significance of *Cupid's Banishment* is found on p. 210.

[97] See Karen Britland, *Drama at the Courts of Henrietta Maria* (New York: Cambridge University Press, 2006), 35-52, and Melinda J. Gough, "Courtly *Comédiantes*: Henrietta Maria and Amateur Women's Stage Plays in France and England," in *Women Players in England, 1500-1660: Beyond the All-Male Stage*, ed. Pamela Allen Brown and Peter Parolin, Studies in Performance and Early Modern Drama (Burlington, VT: Ashgate Publishing, 2005), 193-215. The queen loved to attend the London playhouses as well; Tomlinson, *Women on Stage*, notes that the queen attended four performances at the Blackfriars in the 1630s and one special performance at the Phoenix (11).

in a play"; he must have sighed as he added, "*tempora mutantur et nos*," or "times change, and so must we."[98]

The young queen's French retinue was rather quickly sent back home, but the royal performances continued. In 1633, Walter Montagu's masque, *The Shepherds' Paradise*, was staged, with women again performing speaking roles—the queen played the role of Bellessa, and a majority of the female performers were cross-dressed, playing male roles. It is important to remember, however, that the queen's theatrical performances were private; as the Tuscan representative to the English court reported on one occasion, "The performance was conducted as privately as possible, inasmuch as it is an unusual thing in this country to see the queen upon a stage; the audience consequently was limited to a few of the nobility, expressly invited, no others being admitted."[99]

Nevertheless, the performance of women at the English royal court is widely regarded as in part prompting the anti-theatrical criticism of the London lawyer William Prynne's *Histriomastix*, published in 1633. Prynne condemns the appearance of "women actors on the stage to personate female parts"; in ancient times, he rails, such women were "all notorious impudent, prostituted strumpets." Prynne regards women players — even if they are acting "a female's part"—to be guilty of the "most abominable, unnatural sin of Sodom," just as full of "sodomitical wickedness" as the young male actor who might "put on a woman's apparel, person, and behavior, to act a female's part on the stage." "Both of them," he concludes, "are evil" and "extremely vicious." They are "abominable, both intolerable, neither of them laudatory or necessary, therefore both of them to be abandoned, neither of them to be henceforth tolerated among Christians." [100]

---

[98] The letter of Zoane Pesaro, Venetian ambassador in England, 24 February 1626, and the note of John Chamberlain, 7 March 1626, are quoted in Cerasano and Wynne-Davies, eds, *Renaissance Drama by Women*, 169. I have quietly modernized the spelling and punctuation.

[99] Alessandro Antelminelli to the Grand Duke of Tuscany, 1625/6, quoted in Cerasano and Wynne-Davies, eds., *Renaissance Drama by Women*, 221. I have silently modernized the spelling and punctuation.

[100] William Prynne, *Histrio-mastix: The Players Scourge, or, Actors Tragedie, Divided into Two Parts* . . . (London, 1633), [2]08-16. I have silently modernized the spelling and punctuation. Prynne's condemnation of the theater is massive, more than 1000 pages, followed by an extensive alphabetized "Table . . . of the Chiefest Passages in This Treatise."

His condemnations of female actors point specifically to their public speech as a violation of Christian gender ideology:

> Women . . . with a naked and an uncovered head, speak to the people without shame and usurp impudency to themselves with so great premeditation and infuse so great lasciviousness into the minds of hearers and spectators that all may seem, even with one consent, to extirpate all modesty out of their minds, to disgrace the female nature, and to satiate their lusts with pernicious pleasure. For all things that are done there are absolutely most obscene. For all things . . . (I say) are full of filthy wantonness.

The playhouse itself is a site for all kinds of sin: "whoredoms are there committed," "marriages are there defiled with adulteries," men "are there most unnaturally defiled," and "young men there are effeminate."[101]

Prynne's condemnation of "women actors" was also a response to the first documented appearance of professional actresses on the English stage. Continental women may have performed in England before the mid-seventeenth century—Italian acting companies traveled in England during the reign of Queen Elizabeth, and, as Stephen Orgel notes, "Italian companies always included women."[102] And another hint that women may have performed in England comes from 1608. After traveling in Europe for some months, the Englishman Thomas Coryat reported at great length on the time he spent in Venice, including an account of his visit to a "playhouse," where he saw a comedy. Coryat thought the theater itself was "beggarly" when compared to the "stately playhouses in England." He didn't think the actors or their costumes or the music compared to those in English theaters either, but he admitted that he "observed there" in Venice something that he had never experienced before: "for I saw women act." Significantly, however, Coryat added that although *he* had never seen women actors, he had "heard that it [women acting on stage] hath been sometimes used in London." Coryat was impressed; although he had just said the Venetian actors could not compare to their English counterparts, he said the

---

[101] Prynne, *Histrio-mastix*, 414-15. I have silently modernized the spelling and punctuation.

[102] Orgel, *Impersonations*, 7.

women performed "with as good a grace, action, gesture, and whatsoever convenient for a player as ever I saw any male actor."[103]

While these two references suggest at least the possibility that professional female actors *may* have performed in England late in the sixteenth or early in the seventeenth century, there is no doubt that women *did* perform in London in 1629. They were not *English* actors, however, but French players, who appeared at the Blackfriars Theatre. One Thomas Brande addressed an outraged letter to William Laud, bishop of London, reporting that "certain vagrant French players who had been expelled from their own country, *and those women*, did attempt . . . to act a certain lascivious and unchaste comedy in the French tongue at the Blackfriars." He continued, "Glad I am to say they were hissed, hooted, and pippin-pelted from the stage, so as I do not think they will soon be ready to try the same again." He was wrong about whether they would dare perform again in London, because the actors appeared twice more in commercial playhouses, at the Red Bull and at the Fortune.[104] William Prynne was aware of the same performance, and this was what he condemned in *Histriomastix*. There may well be "female players" in Italy and other "foreign parts," he wrote, but there were also "Frenchwomen actors in a play" who "not long since personated in Blackfriars Playhouse." Contrary to Brande's assertions, Prynne said the women actors were a great attraction, the cause of a "great resort" to the theatre.[105]

Despite outrage like Prynne's, court performances continued, even after the king and queen were forced out of London and relocated to Oxford, and despite the closure of the theaters by parliament in 1642, at the beginning of what would become the first English Civil War.

---

[103] Thomas Coryat, *Coryats Crudities Hastily Gobbled up in Five Months Travels . . .* (London, 1611; rpt. Glasgow: James MacLehose, 1905), 1:386. I have silently modernized the spelling and punctuation. (Coryat also recorded at length his impressions of the "noble and famous courtesans" of the city who attended the performance, privileged to sit "in the best room of all the playhouse," 386-87.)

[104] Thomas Brande's letter is quoted in Orgel, *Impersonations*, 7. Orgel's exploration of the question of why the professional stage in England was all-male—or, as he phrased the question, more provocatively, "Why did the English stage take boys for women?"—begins by noting that women were professional actors in France, Spain, and Italy beginning in the mid-sixteenth century. There was no public theater in the Netherlands (until the mid-seventeenth century) or in Protestant Germany, and so "the English situation is anomalous" (1-2).

[105] Prynne, *Histrio-mastix*, 415. I have silently modernized the spelling and punctuation.

According to Katie Whitaker, "the court continued its prewar artistic life so far as conditions permitted." Actors, set adrift by the closure of the London theaters, "sometimes came into Oxford to perform plays for the court," and the queen herself "kept up the prewar tradition of producing masques for the court's entertainment." However, given the new economic realities, "the scale and grandeur of the proceedings were necessarily reduced." Henrietta Maria was forced to flee to France in 1644, where she received a generous income, and "the full splendor and ceremony of court life resumed," at least for a time.[106] But after the execution of Charles I and the French civil wars of the *Fronde*, there was little occasion—or money—for such light-hearted entertainments. By 1654, the two Stuart princes, Charles and James, were forced to leave France, and they relocated in Cologne. The queen—now the dowager queen mother—retired to the convent of the Sisters of the Visitation of Holy Mary at Chaillot in Paris.[107]

In England, meanwhile, despite the parliamentary ban of 1642 and two further ordinances, issued in 1647 and 1648, the "culture of female acting" did not disappear.[108] Rather, as Sophie Tomlinson argues, the "discontinuance of an all-male stage" seems to have "created new opportunities for women to perform." Women "participate in private house theatricals" during "household entertainments," at country-house parties, and in schools. The playwright and entrepreneur William Davenant even staged a number of "musical entertainments" in London during the Interregnum, including ten days' of "declamations and music" at Rutland House, beginning on 23 May 1656 (though it was his private residence, Davenant opened the performance at Rutland to a limited audience and charged admission). He also produced *The Siege of Rhodes*, generally considered the first English opera, at Rutland House later that year. Crucially, both works included performances by Catherine Coleman, the wife of the composer Edward Coleman. She performed as a member of the chorus in the earlier work but was a lead singer in *The*

---

[106] Whitaker, *Mad Madge*, 50, 58

[107] Henrietta Maria remained in the convent until after the Restoration; at her son Charles II's invitation, she briefly returned to England, but she went back to Paris and the convent in 1665 and died there in 1669.

[108] Ordinance for the suppression of Stage Plays and Interludes within the Cities of London and Westminster and the Counties of Middlesex and Surrey, 22 October 1647, and Ordinance for the suppression of Stage Plays and Interludes with the penalties prescribed for actors and spectators, 11 February 1647/8. In *Acts and Ordinances of the Interregnum, 1642-1660*, ed. Firth and Rait, 1027 and 1070-72.

Siege of Rhodes. In 1658, she performed the same role when *The Siege of Rhodes* was staged at the Cockpit Theatre in Drury Lane.[109]

The history of female performance in England is thus complicated and uncertain. Did women participate in medieval mystery plays? Why were Englishwomen excluded from the professional stage? When did continental actresses first perform in England? What was the public reaction to their appearance on stage? The history of female playwriting, by contrast, is much easier to narrate.

The earliest Englishwoman known to have written a play is Katherine of Sutton, the abbess of Barking Abbey. Not much is known about her, except that she was abbess of the convent from 1363 to 1376. A prefatory note in the surviving manuscript of the Barking play says that it was "instituted" by the abbess in order to "dispel" the "sluggishness" of the "faithful." The composition is a multi-part liturgical drama that focuses on significant events associated with the celebration of Easter: the *Depositio crucis,* a reenactment of the entombment of Christ performed on Good Friday, culminates in the removal of the cross and the host from the altar and their symbolic burial; the *Descensus Christi*, performed at Easter matins, dramatizes the descent of Christ into hell (the "harrowing" of hell), traditionally the time between Jesus's crucifixion and resurrection; the *Elevatio Christi* depicts the restoration of the cross and host to the altar; the *Visitatio sepulchri*, played directly after the *Descensus* and the *Elevatio*, reenacts the early-morning visit to the empty tomb of the "three Marys," Mary, the mother of Jesus, Mary Magdalene, and Mary Salome, a follower of Jesus, sometimes identified as the mother of two of the apostles, James and John. The play was written for performance by both friars and, as we have noted above, by nuns. Its audience included the nuns themselves (probably between thirty-five and forty women) as well as lay men and women who came to the convent's church for the celebration of Easter. The manuscript contains fairly extensive "stage" directions that give some sense of the performance.[110]

---

[109] On new performing opportunities for women and for the significance of Catherine Coleman, see Tomlinson, *Women on Stage*, 156-57. On William Davenant's "entertainments" staged during the Interregnum, see Dale B. J. Randall, *Winter Fruit: English Drama, 1642-1660* (Lexington: The University of Kentucky Press, 1995), 169-79.

[110] On Katherine of Sutton, see Cotton, *Women Playwrights in England*, 27-28, and her earlier "Katherine of Sutton: The First English Woman Playwright," *Educational Theatre Journal* 30, no. 4 (1978): 475–81. See also Michael O'Connell, "Katherine of

Nearly two centuries pass before we find another dramatic text written by a woman, a translation of Euripides' *Iphigenia* made by Lady Jane Lumley (c. 1537-1576), the daughter of Henry Fitzalan, earl of Arundel, and Katherine Grey.[111] Carefully educated by her father—she knew both Latin and Greek—Jane had access to his extensive library; after her marriage to John, baron Lumley, she could also enjoy the exceptional library at Lumley Castle. (Her father's library was later inherited by her husband.) It was after her 1550 marriage, at some point between 1553 and 1557, that Jane Lumley completed *The Tragedy of Euripides called Iphigeneia*, more likely working from a Greek-Latin translation by the Dutch scholar Desiderius Erasmus than from the Greek original.[112] While earlier generations of literary critics regarded Lumley's work as a purely academic exercise, one that enabled a teenage girl to show off her privileged education, Patricia Demars identifies it as a paraphrase rather than a close (and plodding) translation: "Here is Euripides filtered through the eyes of a widely read, capable, protected early modern young woman, whose domestic idiom, distinctive word choices, misconstruals, deliberate exclusions and sometimes softened,

---

Sutton," in *Women's Works*, vol. 1: *900-1550*, ed. Donald W. Foster (New York: Wicked Good Books, 2013), 49-50. Following the brief essay on the abbess is "The Easter Play of the Nuns of Barking Convent," trans. Michael O'Connell, 51-53.

[111] Katherine Grey was the daughter of Thomas Grey, first marquis of Dorset; Katherine Grey's brother, Thomas Grey, second marquis of Dorset, was the grandfather of Lady Jane Grey, a formidable scholar and the so-called Nine Days' Queen.

[112] Diane Purkiss argues for a date of 1553, the year that Jane's father acquired the confiscated library of Thomas Cranmer, which included two copies of the play by Euripides. On this see Purkiss, ed., *Three Tragedies by Renaissance Women: "The Tragedie of Iphigeneia," "The Tragedie of Antonie," "The Tragedie of Mariam,"* Penguin Dramatists (Harmondsworth, UK: Penguin Books, 1998), xxiv-xxv. Marion Wynne-Davies believes that the play was translated in 1557, when Lumley and her husband were at Nonsuch, the royal palace sold by Mary Tudor to Lumley's father in 1556. See Wynne-Davies, "The Good Lady Lumley's Desire: *Iphigeneia* and the Nonsuch Banqueting House," in *Heroines of the Golden StAge: Women and Drama in Spain and England 1500-1700*, ed. Rina Walthaus and Marguérite Corporaal (Kassel, Germany: Reichenberger, 2008), 111-128.

On Lumley, her education, and her play, see Marta Straznicky, *Privacy, Playreading, and Women's Closet Drama, 1550-1700* (New York: Cambridge University Press, 2004), 19-47.

sometimes heightened tragic details convey the blended experience of the Greek and Latin texts."[113]

And rather than a juvenile exercise, the play is surely intended as a complex political allegory. If the translation dates to 1553, it would have been completed after Jane Grey's brief "reign" as queen of England but before her execution—Lumley was related to Jane Grey through her mother, but Lumley's father played an important role in supporting Mary Tudor's claim to the throne, and he would sign the warrant for Jane Grey's execution in 1554. Iphigenia's willing and dignified self-sacrifice may thus represent Jane Grey's necessary death, which preserved the security of England and the Catholic faith.[114] If the translation were completed in 1556 or 1557, after Elizabeth Tudor became queen, it might be read as a kind of exoneration of Arundel. In this context, as Marion Wynne-Davies argues, the play's "dramatic discourse allowed [Jane Lumley] to display the power and cultural sophistication of her father, while simultaneously presenting his actions as part of a wider necessity, perhaps even encouraging him to adopt such a stance as a new Protestant queen ascended the throne." Whatever the work's political context, Lumley "wisely chose to employ the cautious dramatic form of household theater" for her drama.[115] Her audience, while educated and privileged, is limited—a small group confined to her familial and social sphere.

Queen Elizabeth also produced a dramatic work, although an incomplete one. The Tudor queen's translation, from a play by Seneca, was probably undertaken in 1589. The 123 lines from *Hercules on Oeta* come from a choral ode in the second act of the Latin original. The chorus of Aetolian women has just realized that the robe sent to Hercules by his wife is poisoned. Elizabeth's reworking of the chorus is "less a translation, strictly conceived, than an imitation," a version in which she omits the part of the original that focuses on unhappy wives, concentrating instead on "the chorus's reflections on the vulnerability of monarchs and other eminent persons to the treachery of fellow mortals

---

[113] Demars, "On First Looking into Lumley's Euripides," *Renaissance and Reformation* n.s. 23, no. 1 (1999): 38.

[114] See Demars, "On First Looking," *passim*.

[115] Wynne-Davies, "The Theater," *British Women's Writing*, 2:184. In addition to the Purkiss edition of Lumley's play, a significant portion of the play, in a modern English translation, is in *Women's Works*, vol. 2: *1550-1603*, ed. Donald W. Foster, (New York: Wicked Good Books, 2014), 24-30, the selection introduced and edited by Foster.

and the vicissitudes of Fortune."[116] Once again we may see a woman using a dramatic text as a way of responding to political tragedy. Janel Mueller and Joshua Scodel read this speech, and the "exceptional volubility and freedom" with which Elizabeth approaches the original, as a means of "debating with herself over signing the warrant" for the execution of Mary Stuart, queen of Scotland. Even the recent victory over the Spanish Armada had not eliminated the threats to England, Elizabeth's continued anxiety perhaps triggering her reflection on the "agonizing dilemma" she had already faced and overcome as well as her "continuing apprehension" that England would once again face a Spanish invasion.[117]

Only two early-modern women, Mary Sidney Herbert and Elizabeth Cary, were able to publish their plays. In the case of Mary Sidney Herbert, countess of Pembroke (1561-1621), her elite status undoubtedly made publication possible, while her political ends made publication desirable. Sidney's 1592 *Antonius, A Tragoedie* was, at least ostensibly, a translation of the French poet Robert Garnier's *Marc-Antoine*, a Senecan tragedy written between 1574 and 1575 and included in his 1585 collected *Tragedies*.[118] As the 1592 title page describes Sidney's *Antonius*, the play was "done in English by the countess of Pembroke." And although public performances of professional actors like Pembroke's Men, under the patronage of her husband, Henry Herbert, in London playhouses like the Theatre, the Curtain, and the Swan, were by this time well established, Sidney's play was not written to be performed before large urban audiences in such theaters, but was

---

[116] Elizabeth I, *Translations, 1544-1589*, ed. Janel Mueller and Joshua Scodel (Chicago: University of Chicago Press, 2008), 442. Mueller and Scodel date Elizabeth's translation based on the publication of the edition of Seneca that seems to have been the queen's source, Lucius Annaeus Seneca, *Tragoediae* (London, 1589). In addition to the text in Mueller and Scodel, 439-56, Elizabeth's *Hercules Oetaeus* is in Cerasano and Wynne-Davies, eds., *Renaissance Drama by Women*, 7-12. A selection is also included in Foster, ed., *Women's Works*, 2:107.

[117] Mueller and Scodel, eds., *Translations*, 444.

[118] Garnier's play was first published in 1578 then republished in *Les Tragédies* (Paris, 1585). Textual evidence indicates Sidney used the 1585 revised version of the play. On this see Barry Weller, "Mary Sidney, countess of Pembroke: *Antonius*," in *The Ashgate Research Companion to the Sidneys, 1500-1700*, vol. 2, *Literature*, ed. Margaret P. Hannay, Mary Ellen Lamb, and Michael G. Brennan (Burlington, VT: Ashgate Publishing, 2015), 199.

Sidney's play was first published in a volume that began with her *Discourse of Life and Death* . . . (London, 1592), the play appearing as second item in the book.

instead, like Lumley's *Iphigeneia,* "intended" for private "staged readings" or household performance and thus restricted to an exclusive coterie audience.

Publication, however, moved Sidney's play from the private realm into the public sphere. In her choice of a text and in her decision to publish, her motivations seem to have been political, a way to further the Protestant political program of the Sidney family, most notably of her brother, the poet and courtier Sir Philip Sidney; in Margaret Hannay's opinion, "When Mary Sidney made her decision to translate a work by Robert Garnier, a magistrate who used his drama to criticize the state, she was making a political statement."[119] In Sidney's focus on the character of Cleopatra and in the powerful, extended speeches of the Egyptian queen, she could promote a view of female heroism and fidelity even while demonstrating "the dangers of civil war, stressing the need for rulers to fulfil[l] their obligations to their subjects and not to allow passion to cloud their judgements."[120] Sidney's play proved popular—it appeared in two additional printings in 1595, under the revised title of *The Tragedie of Antonie,* with three more printings before 1607.[121] (By contrast, Jane Lumley's *Iphigeneia* was not published until 1909.[122])

Equally daring in her decision to publish was Elizabeth Tanfield Cary (1585-1639), the first Englishwoman known to have written an original play. Her *Tragedy of Mariam, the Fair Queen of Jewry* dramatizes the story of Herod, the king of Judea, and his wife, Mariam. In his jealousy and rage, Herod has his wife murdered, prompting frequent comparisons between Cary's play and Shakespeare's *Othello.* Cary's source was Thomas Lodge's 1602 *Antiquities of the Jews,* his translation of the Jewish historian Titus Flavius Josephus's first-century history of the Jews; her play was

---

[119] Margaret Hannay, *Philip's Phoenix: Mary Sidney, Countess of Pembroke* (New York: Oxford University Press, 1990), 126-27.

[120] Cerasano and Wynne-Davies, eds., *Renaissance Drama by Women,* 17.

[121] Cerasano and Wynne-Davies, eds., *Renaissance Drama by Women,* 16. The text of *Antonie* is available in Purkiss, ed., *Three Tragedies by Renaissance Women,* and in Cerasano and Wynne-Davies, eds., *Renaissance Drama by Women.* The first modern publication of the play was by Alice H. Luce, *The Countess of Pembroke's "Antonie"* (Weimar: Emil Felber, 1897). One further Sidney dramatic piece may be noted here. Mary Sidney Herbert's pastoral "Dialogue between Two Shepherds, Thenot and Piers, in Praise of Astrea" was probably written for Elizabeth I's planned visit to Wilton in 1599. The visit did not take place, but the dialogue was printed in Francis Davison's *A Poetical Rapsody* (London, 1602).

[122] Jane Lumley, trans., *Iphigenia at Aulis,* ed. Harold H. Child (London: Malone Society, 1909).

probably completed between 1602, when, at the age of fifteen, she was married to Henry Cary, later Viscount Falkland, and 1604. (Shakespeare's *Othello* is dated to about the same period, its first recorded performance for King James's court at Whitehall on 1 November 1604.) As Cary's daughter would later write, Henry Cary left immediately after the wedding to continue his military career in the Low Countries, the newly married Elizabeth remaining, at first, with her own family. But his mother, Catherine Knevet Cary, soon insisted on "having" her son's wife in her custody, though Cary's daughter wrote that the young, newly married Elizabeth was "used" very "hardly" and confined "to her chamber" in her husband's family home. Cary seemed not to have minded too much, entertaining herself happily with reading, until her mother-in-law "took away all her books, with command to have no more brought her."[123] Undaunted, and deprived of books to read, the young woman began to write. Among her compositions seems to have been an earlier tragedy, now lost, set in Syracuse—in a poem written in praise of Cary, the English poet John Davies would later refer to Cary not only as his pupil but to her *two* plays "of state," one set in Syracuse, the other in Palestine (the setting of *Mariam*). When Cary published *Mariam* in 1613, she added a dedicatory sonnet, in which she alludes to her "first" play, set in Sicily and "consecrated to Apollo."[124]

When Cary published her work, she did not have the protection of the kind of title Mary Sidney had—Sidney presented herself in her publications not as Mary Sidney Herbert, but as "the countess of Pembroke." But Cary found other ways to protect her identity, first by insisting on the quality of her character ("written by that learned, virtuous, and truly noble lady"), then shielding herself by using only her initials ("E. C."). And the reasons for Cary's caution are clear—nowhere

---

[123] *The Lady Falkland: Her Life*, by "one of her daughters," in Elizabeth Cary, the lady Falkland, *The Tragedy of Mariam, the Fair Queen of Jewry, with "The Lady Falkland: Her Life" by One of Her Daughters*, ed. Barry Weller and Margaret W. Ferguson (Berkeley: University of California Press, 1994), 188-89.

[124] John Davies, *The Muses Sacrifice, or Divine Meditations* (London, 1612), in S. P. Cerasano and Marion Wynne-Davies, eds., *Readings in Renaissance Women's Drama: Criticism, History, and Performance, 1594-1998* (New York: Routledge, 1998), 13-14. Cary's sonnet is in *The Tragedie of Mariam, the Faire Queene of Jewry* (London, 1613), n. p. *The Tragedy of Mariam* was not published again until the early twentieth century: A. C. Dunstan, ed., *The Tragedy of Mariam, 1613*, Malone Society Reprints (Oxford: Oxford University Press, 1914). Cary's dedicatory sonnet and the play are in Weller and Hannay's edition; in Cerasano and Wynne-Davies, eds., *Renaissance Drama*; and in Purkiss, ed., *Three Tragedies by Renaissance Women*.

is the danger of women's public speech, and, by extension, publication, more starkly presented than in *Mariam*. In the first line of her opening soliloquy, Mariam acknowledges the fault of her "public voice," moving quickly to condemn her own speech as "too rash." "Unbridled speech is Mariam's worst disgrace," Herod's chief counselor observes. The chorus, too, comments on Mariam's public speech: even the most virtuous of women is not free from suspicion if she speaks openly and publicly. It's not enough to *be* chaste, the chorus warns, a woman must *behave* circumspectly, "by her proper self restrained." To speak openly is to "blot" her "glory": "That wife her hand against her fame doth rear, / That more than to her lord alone will give / A private word to any second ear." Though "most chaste," such a wife "wounds her honour." And then, the ultimate warning: "Her mind if not peculiar is not chaste, / For in a wife it is no worse to find, / A common body than a common mind." Or, as Herod puts it crudely before having Mariam killed, "She's unchaste; / Her mouth will open to every stranger's ear."[125] Even so, Cary did publish her play, perhaps encouraged by Davies's warning that if she gave her "works both birth and grave," those in "times to come" would not be able to "credit" the accomplishments of the "weaker sex"—nor would Cary's "wit and grace" have earned her "fame."[126] Marion Wynne-Davies writes that, among all these early women dramatists—Lumley, Sidney, even the queen herself—

it is Cary who most acknowledges the limitations that constrained a sixteenth-century Englishwoman writing a dramatic text, namely: that they could hardly hope for a performance of their work, that propriety and convention ensured that they would have no audience, and that they had no access to a public stage. . . . Elizabeth Cary . . . took the negation of voice, action, and space to its absurd conclusion, produc[ing] not only a stringent condemnation of the repression of women, but also an early modern parable of tyranny, rebellion, and subjugation.[127]

---

[125] Cary, *Mariam*, in Cerasano and Wynne-Davies, eds., *Renaissance Drama by Women*, 1.1, 6; 3.183-84, 219-50; 4.432-33.

[126] Davies, *The Muses Sacrifice*, in Cerasano and Wynne-Davies, eds., *Readings in Renaissance Women's Drama*, 14.

[127] Wynne-Davies, "The Theater," in *The History of British Women's Writing*, 2:193.

After Elizabeth Cary, women in England seem to fall mostly silent, at least when it comes to writing drama. Mostly, but not entirely. Mary Sidney Herbert's niece, Mary Sidney Wroth (1587-1651?), has the distinction of being the first Englishwoman to write an original comedy, *Love's Victory*, probably composed about 1620, but it was not published. Her decision to write a dramatic work is understandable. Not only had she performed in court masques, she had probably attended performances at public theaters.[128] But Wroth had a more important precedent, her aunt's *Tragedie of Antonie*, and, also like her aunt, Wroth probably intended her play for readings with, and perhaps performance by, family and friends.

While many readings of Wroth's *Love's Victory* (and of her romance, *Urania*) focus on the way Wroth dramatizes the complex romantic relationships of the Sidney family, it may also be the case that the allegory of *Love's Victory* is political as well as personal. Marion Wynne-Davies argues that the lovers Musella and Philisses represent *both* Wroth and her lover/cousin William Herbert *and* Elizabeth Stuart and her husband, Frederick V, elector palatine of the Rhine. Despite Queen Anna of Denmark's opposition to the match, the young Stuart princess was married to the equally young prince palatine in a lavish ceremony at Whitehall in 1613, the play expressing the support of the Sidney family for the match. Akiko Kusonoki, however, argues that the play's "political import" might be slightly different, suggesting the play was written later, in 1619, when the young couple was being offered the crown of Bohemia. While King James opposed the offer, the play represented the support and encouragement of the Sidney-Herbert family circle, "an appeal in particular to female members to be active in promoting Protestant policy to help the couple" who were "wavering" about whether to accept the crown, given the English king's objections.[129] It is

---

[128] On Lady Mary Wroth's performance in Jacobean masques, see above, 33. Josephine Roberts concludes that Wroth had also attended performances in playhouses, "as suggested by her references to the theater in the *Urania*." Roberts, ed., *The Poems of Lady Mary Wroth*, 53. Wroth's *Love's Victory* is in Cerasano and Wynne-Davies, eds., *Renaissance Drama by Women*.

[129] On *Love's Victory* as historical allegory, in particular focused on Elizabeth Stuart's marriage, see Marion Wynne-Davies, *Women Writers and Familial Discourse in the English Renaissance: Relative Values*, Early Modern Literature in History (New York: Palgrave Macmillan, 2007), 102-3. For the view that the play encourages the young couple to accept the crown of Bohemia, see Akiko Kusonoki, "Wroth's *Love's Victory* as a Response to Shakespeare's Representation of Gender Distinctions: With Special

also possible that Wroth's play might have moved beyond the Sidney family circle, perhaps "staged" for amateur performances.[130] But *Love's Victory* was not published for more than two hundred years, and even then it was not published in its entirety—the great (and somewhat notorious) nineteenth-century scholar, antiquarian researcher, and editor James Halliwell[-Phillips] noted that he had discovered the play in manuscript, and while he had originally believed it to be "worth printing," he ultimately decided that it was not "of sufficient interest for publication, when a minute examination came to be made." Instead of the whole play, he concluded that only "brief extracts" were worthy of publication.[131]

Finally, and from our point of view much closer to home, is *The Concealed Fancies*, a play written by Elizabeth Cavendish Brackley and Jane

---

Reference to *Romeo and Juliet*," in *Mary Wroth and Shakespeare*, Routledge Studies in Shakespeare, ed. Paul Salzman and Marion Wynne-Davies (New York: Routledge, 2015), 81.

Elizabeth Stuart and Frederick V, elector of Palatine, became king and queen of Bohemia for just one winter, Frederick crowned as king on 4 November 1619, Elizabeth as queen three days later. By November of the next year, their reign was over.

[130] A copy of *Love's Victory* is known to have belonged to Sir Edward Dering, an English politician and antiquarian who collected many play texts and arranged for amateur theatrical performances with his family and friends. The possibility that Dering, an "intimate friend" of Mary Sidney Wroth's brother, Robert Sidney, may have "staged" a performance of *Love's Victory* in the 1620s is suggested by Michael G. Brennan, ed., *Love's Victory* (London: The Roxburghe Club, 1988), 13-15. See also Cerasano and Wynne-Davies, eds., *Renaissance Drama by Women*, 93. The possibility of a performance staged by Dering is also discussed by Stephanie Hodgson-Wright, "Beauty, Chastity, and Wit: Feminising the Centre-Stage," in *Women and Dramatic Production, 1550-1700*, Longman Medieval and Renaissance Library, ed. Alison Findlay, Stephanie Hodgson-Wright, and Gweno Williams (New York: Routledge, 2000), 59.

[131] "Extracts" from "an unpublished MS. Drama of the Seventeenth Century, entitled *Love's Victorie*" were included in James O. Halliwell, ed., *A Brief Description of the Ancient and Modern Manuscripts Preserved in the Public Library, Plymouth, to Which Are Added, Some Fragments of Early Literature, Hitherto Unprinted* (London, 1853), 212-36. The comments are from p. 212. Halliwell concludes his extract by saying that the dramatist James Shirley had written a play "now perished" with the title *Love's Victory*, but "the internal evidence would scarcely lead us to believe that this is one of his productions" (236). Halliwell is undoubtedly an important scholar, but also an unscrupulous "editor" who cut up seventeenth-century books and was accused of stealing books from the collection of Trinity College, Cambridge. After 1872, he added the family name of his wife, Phillipps, to his own.

Cavendish.[132] Elizabeth (1616-63) and Jane (1621-69) were the children of William Cavendish's first marriage. While William Cavendish was serving as a general with the royalist forces during the first Civil War, his wife, Elizabeth Bassett, and their daughters (including a third daughter, Frances) remained behind at Welbeck Abbey, which served as a garrison for the army loyal to the king. After Elizabeth Bassett died in 1643, William Cavendish's daughters remained at Welbeck, offering what help they could to the royalist cause—Jane, in particular, seems to have acted as a kind of agent for the king, sending whatever information she could come by to him. Welbeck was surrendered to the parliamentary army in August of 1644, but the young women remained there, under the protection of the commander of the garrison; after the abbey's surrender, the victorious earl of Manchester wrote that he had "engaged" himself "for their quiet abode."[133] Welbeck was briefly recaptured by the king in 1645, but was finally turned over to the parliamentary forces for good in November of 1645.

William Cavendish's daughters seem to have written *The Concealed Fancies* during the time they were under siege in their family home. The play's main plot involves two young women, Luceny and Tattiney, the daughters of Lord Calsindow. These two well-educated and witty young women refuse to marry their suitors until the young men have been effectively "tamed." In the play's subplot, three young women are under siege in the castle of Bellamo, where they must endure their "captivity," separated from their lovers, the sons of Lord Calsindow. While they are in Bellamo, they pass the time by acting out plays, including one about Cleopatra "when she was in her captivity," though their plays are not presented as plays-within-the-play—we only hear about these entertainments, we don't see them. The three young women are finally released from Bellamo when the siege is lifted, and they are reunited with their lovers; Luceny and Tattiney, too, end the play as married women.

Even without the play-within-a-play device, *The Concealed Fancies* embeds one story within another, with the Cavendish sisters, under siege in Welbeck, writing a play about young women under siege—Elizabeth and Jane give their besieged heroines the happy ending that they haven't

---

[132] Elizabeth Cavendish Brackley and Jane Cavendish, *The Concealed Fancies*, is in Cerasano and Wynne-Davies, eds., *Renaissance Drama by Women*.

[133] Edward Montagu, earl of Manchester, letter of August 1644, quoted in Nathan Comfort Starr, "*The Concealed Fansyes*: A Play by Lady Jane Cavendish and Lady Elizabeth Brackley," *PMLA* 46, no. 3 (1931): 813.

yet achieved for themselves. They might also have been writing in response to their father's relationship to the young Margaret Lucas. S. P. Cerasano and Marion Wynne-Davies suggest that the duke's daughters satirize their future stepmother in the character of Lady Tranquility, a vain old woman who is in love with Lord Calsindow but who, at the play's end, is married off to Corpolent, a suitor whom Luceny has rejected.[134] But, while Lady Tranquility might be old, Margaret Lucas was not—and she didn't get passed off to a fat boob, either.[135]

This, then, is the context for Margaret Cavendish as she began writing her plays in the 1650s: between 1558, about the time Jane Lumley translated *Iphigeneia*, and 1642, when the theaters were closed (just about the time Jane and Elizabeth Cavendish wrote *Love's Victory*), some 2,000 to 3,000 plays were written and performed by Englishmen. Of this number, about 650 plays survive.[136] In contrast to the thousands of plays written by men, only a handful of dramatic texts are known to have been written by women, including Elizabeth Tudor's fragment. And during this period, only two plays written by women were published. Understanding this context is essential to assessing the enormity of Margaret Cavendish's accomplishment in writing and publishing two collections of plays.

Whether Cavendish might have had access to Mary Sidney's *Tragedie of Antonie* or Elizabeth Cary's *Tragedy of Mariam* is unknown. Aside from her reading of Shakespeare and her youthful experience of seeing plays in London, she does not write much about her familiarity with dramatic performance, at least not in her autobiography. If Cavendish saw the plays and masques performed for Henrietta Maria when she was with the queen in Oxford or in Paris, she does not write about them. She mentions only her painful shyness: "I neither heeded what was said or practiced but just what belonged to my loyal duty and my own honest

[134] Cerasano and Wynne-Davies, eds. *Renaissance Drama by Women*, 129.

[135] The Cavendish sisters' play was not published until Nathan Comfort Starr's 1931 transcription in "*The Concealed Fansyes*: A Play by Lady Jane Cavendish and Lady Elizabeth Brackley," 802-38.

[136] For this number see W. W. Greg, ed., *Henslowe's Diary* (London, 1904-8), 2:146, cited also by G. K. Hunter, *English Drama 1586-1642: The Age of Shakespeare*, vol. 6 of *The Oxford History of English Literature* (Oxford: Clarendon Press, 1997), 3n6. The records for one London company—the Admiral's Men—show that between 1594 and 1602 "some 230 plays [were] paid for and (usually) performed"; during the same period, the Chamberlain's/King's men paid for 289 plays (Hunter, 362-63).

reputation."[137] But in marrying William Cavendish, Margaret found a husband who was interested in plays, performance, and playwriting. Before the Civil Wars sent him into exile on the continent, he had staged household performances, including two for Charles I and Henrietta Maria, one at Welbeck Abbey, the other at Bolsover Castle.[138] He is also well known for his financial support of the playwrights Ben Jonson and James Shirley, who may have had a hand in William Cavendish's *The Country Captain*, performed by the King's Men at the Blackfriars Theatre between 1639 and 1642. This play was published in 1649 along with a second, *The Varietie*, both attributed on the title page to "a person of honor."[139] Another play by William Cavendish, *The Humorous Lovers*, was first performed in 1667, although, as we have seen, when Samuel Pepys saw the play he thought it was by *Margaret* Cavendish.[140] A fourth play, *The Triumphant Widow*, was published in 1677; it had been performed in 1674 by the King's Men—in the words of the title page, "acted by His Royal Highness's Servants"—its authorship attributed to "His Grace, the duke of Newcastle."[141] One further play, *Sir Martin Mar-all*, was also attributed to William Cavendish; when the play was entered in the

---

[137] Cavendish, *True Relation*, in Firth, ed., *Life of William Cavendish*, 160. I have silently modernized the spelling and punctuation.

[138] Margaret Cavendish, *Life of . . . William Cavendishe . . .* , in Firth, ed., *Life of William Cavendish*, 103-4. See also Julie Crawford, "'Pleaders, Atturneys, Petitioners and the like': Margaret Cavendish and the Dramatic Petition," in *Women Players in England*, ed. Brown and Parolin, 243.

[139] *The Country Captain and The Varietie, Two Comedies* (London, 1649). Samuel Pepys saw *The Country Captain* when it was revived in London after the Restoration. About the 26 October 1661 performance by the King's Company, he wrote that it was "the first time it hath been acted this twenty-five years, . . . but so silly a play as in all my life I never saw, and the first that ever I was weary of in my life." I have silently modernized the spelling and punctuation. Wearied or not, he saw the play again on 25 November 1661, on 14 August 1667, and on 14 May 1668. His view of the play did not change. For these references see Pepys, in *The Diary of Samuel Pepys . . .* , ed. Henry B. Wheatley (New York: Macmillan, 1893), 2:118, 2:134; and *The Diary of Samuel Pepys . . .* , ed. Henry B. Wheatley (New York: Macmillan, 1896), 7:67-68 and 8:16.

[140] *The Humorous Lovers, a Comedy* (London, 1677). For Pepys's view of this play, see above, n. 77.

[141] *The Triumphant Widow, or the Medley of Humours, A Comedy* (London, 1677). Although attributed to William Cavendish, the playwright Thomas Shadwell seems to have collaborated on *The Triumphant Widow*.

On William Cavendish's plays, see also Lynn Hulse, ed., *William Cavendish: Dramatic Works*, Malone Society Reprints 158 (Oxford: Oxford University Press, 1996). Hulse publishes twenty-three previously unpublished "dramatic pieces," including fragments, scenes, a masque, and several play songs.

Stationer's Register in 1666, his authorship was noted. Performed at the Duke of York's Playhouse and at court for some thirty performances in 1668 and 1669, it was an enormous success. The play was published anonymously in 1668 and in a 1678 second edition, but the 1691 third edition listed the author as John Dryden; Cavendish's "authorship" of this play may have rested on his translation of *L'Étourdi* by Molière, on which *Sir Martin Mar-all* was based.[142]

In 1646, when Henrietta Maria was in Paris, Prince Charles, later Charles II, joined his mother; while there, he maintained a group of actors. In her biography of Margaret Cavendish, Katie Whitaker indicates that William Cavendish "was among those who wrote pieces" for the prince's company. Reports about William's writing for such frivolous purposes reached England and were commented on in *The Kingdom's Weekly Intelligencer: Sent Abroad to Prevent Misinformation*, a parliamentary newspaper. That William Cavendish would participate in such an activity "showed in him either an admirable temper and settledness of mind," the writer sniffed, "or else an infinite and vain affection unto poetry, that in the ruins of his country and himself he can be at leisure to make prologues and epilogues for players."[143] Margaret may also have seen theatrical performances at the Palais Royal during the Cavendishes' Parisian exile—when she came to write her own plays she would embed in one of them a criticism of Italian and French plays, or at least of Italian and French actors.[144]

After the Cavendishes left Paris in 1648, they moved on briefly to Rotterdam. William Cavendish may already have been at work preparing *The Country Captain* and *The Variety* for publication; Margaret would later write about her appreciation of her husband's plays and his "performance" of them for her, as his audience. She also believed her husband to be "the best lyric and dramatic poet of his age."[145] Once they moved on to Antwerp, the couple visited the duchess of Lorraine at Beersel Castle, where there were theaters catering to English exiles and where they could also see plays and masques performed by the duchess's

---

[142] The indefatigable Pepys saw this play numerous times as well and enjoyed it immensely.

[143] Quoted in Whitaker, *Mad Madge*, 88. I have silently modernized the spelling and punctuation.

[144] This criticism appears in *The Female Academy*, 4.2.

[145] Cavendish, *Life of . . . William Cavendishe . . .* , in Firth, ed., *Life of William Cavendish*, 108-9.

courtiers.[146] In Antwerp, William Cavendish staged a number of entertainments, including pastorals, at Rubens House, where the couple lived from late in 1648 until their return to England in 1660.[147] It was during their residence in Antwerp that Cavendish began writing her "sociable letters." In one of her early letters, she—or, rather, the writer who addresses an unnamed female correspondent—professes not to care much about attending plays. While emphasizing her love of "retirement," a life of "calm silence" where she can live "free from disturbance" and in peace, "Cavendish" names attending plays as one of the activities she avoids. "I do not go personally to masques, balls, and plays," she writes, "yet my thoughts entertain my mind with such pleasures, for some of my thoughts make plays, and others act those plays on the stage of imagination, where my mind sits as a spectator."[148] Perhaps her playwriting began with these pleasant thoughts, for she suggests as much in her verse dedication to the 1662 *Plays*:

To those that do delight in scenes and wit
I dedicate my book, for those I writ,
Next to my own delight, for I did take
Much pleasure and delight these plays to make,
For all the time my plays a-making were,
My brain the stage, my thoughts were acting there.[149]

But the letter-writer is not completely uninterested in public performance, however, as she spends a considerable amount of time in a later letter describing the variety of "sights and shows" that could be seen in Antwerp: "dancers on the ropes," tumblers, jugglers, "private stage-players," mountebanks, "monsters," and beasts among them. She

---

[146] Whitaker, *Mad Madge*, 119-21.

[147] Designed by Peter Paul Rubens, it had been the artist's home; the Cavendishes rented it from his widow. For a description of the house and grounds, see Grant, *Margaret the First*, 133-35; Jones, *A Glorious Fame*, 71-73; and Whitaker, *Mad Madge*, 108-109. The Grant and Whitaker biographies include courtyard views of the house, but Jones reproduces multiple images, including interiors and grounds.

[148] Cavendish, Letter 29, *Sociable Letters*, 56-57. I have silently modernized the spelling and punctuation. Cavendish did not publish her *Sociable Letters* until 1664, after the Cavendishes returned to England, but they were written while she was living in Antwerp.

[149] Cavendish, "Dedication," *Playes*, A2r. I have silently modernized the spelling and punctuation.

is quick to add, however, that she doesn't "take the pains to see them," except for a few. Among those "few" she admits to making an effort to see is one of the "monsters" she mentions, a woman at a carnival whom Cavendish describes as "like a shag-dog, not in shape but hair, as grown all over her body."[150] Cavendish is disturbed by the "strangeness" of this "dog-like creature." "It troubled my mind a long time," she writes.[151]

She also describes watching an Italian mountebank, accompanied by several actors, who performed upon an "open stage." "Cavendish" notes that the mountebank drew lots of people around to "hear him tell the virtues, or rather lies, of his drugs, cures, and skill," clearly hoping to "persuade them to buy and to be cozened and deceived, both in words, drugs, and money," but she is more interested in the performers accompanying him—in particular a fool and "two handsome women actors, both sisters," one the wife of the mountebank, one the wife of the actor playing the fool. Cavendish writes that the fool's wife "was the best female actor that ever I saw." The women were clearly cross-dressed and playing men's roles. Cavendish adds, "for acting a man's part, she did it so naturally as if she had been of that sex, and yet she was of a neat, slender shape, but being in her doublet and breeches, and a sword hanging by her side, one would have believed she never had worn a petticoat and had been more used to handle a sword than a distaff." So pleased was Cavendish with this performance, that she hired a room in a house "and went every day to see them" until they were forced to leave town, to her "great grief." And then, "they being gone, I was troubled for the loss of that pastime which I took in seeing them act; wherefore to please me, my fancy set up a stage in my brain."[152]

---

[150] "Having shaggy hair. Formerly sometimes hyphened, as *shag-dog*" (*OED*).

[151] M. A. Katritzky suggests Margaret Cavendish may have seen the harpsichordist Barbara Urslerin, "the only sufferer of hypertrichosis born in seventeenth-century Europe known to have survived into adulthood," whose "Bavarian parents showed her around European fairgrounds for money from earliest infanthood." She continued touring in adulthood with her husband/manager. Katritzky, "'A Wonderfull Monster Borne in Germany': Hairy Girls in Medieval and Early Modern German Book, Court and Performance Culture," *German Life and Letters* 67, no. 4 (2014), http://www.ncbi.nlm.nih.gov/pmc/articles/PMC4296693/. See also Katritzky, "Introduction: 'Mountebanks, Monsters, and Several Beasts': Margaret Cavendish at the Antwerp Carnival Fair," *Women, Medicine and Theatre, 1500-1850: Literary Mountebanks and Performing Quacks*, Studies in Performance and Early Modern Drama (Burlington, VT: Ashgate, 2007), 1-22.

[152] Cavendish, Letter 195, *Sociable Letters*, 405-8. I have silently modernized the spelling and punctuation.

While Cavendish may profess a preference for imagined performances over the reality of performance—at least most of the time—she did write at some length about Shakespeare in one of her letters. Her observations are not shallow; indeed, from the number of characters she mentions, it is clear that she has great familiarity with the body of Shakespeare's work. But it is also clear that she is not so much interested in Shakespeare on stage as she is Shakespeare on the page—"there is not any person he hath described in his book, but his readers might think they were well acquainted with them," she writes. And, again, while arguing that those who "dispraised his plays" were envious rather than offering valid criticism, she adds, "for those that could read his plays could not be so foolish to condemn them."[153] Notably, for all the ridicule and criticism she received in her lifetime, Cavendish is today credited for having published the first critical essay on Shakespeare and his work—"she anticipates Dryden in being the first to give a general prose assessment of Shakespeare as a dramatist."[154]

Margaret Cavendish and the Folio Tradition

In 1662, when Margaret Cavendish decided to publish a collection of her plays, she was participating in a genre not particularly welcoming to women; at the same time, she also decided to present her dramatic work in a format that had only recently been adopted for plays written by men—men who had dominated the Elizabethan and Jacobean stages, the "Triumvirate of Wit," Ben Jonson, William Shakespeare, and the collaborative writing partners Francis Beaumont and John Fletcher.[155] As a woman writer, Cavendish had few precedents for the publication of her dramatic work. Mary Sidney Herbert had been the first woman to publish a play, and when *Antonius* appeared in 1592, in the same volume

---

[153] Cavendish, Letter 123, *Sociable Letters*, 246-7. I have silently modernized the spelling and punctuation.

[154] G. Blakemore Evans et al., eds., *The Riverside Shakespeare* (Princeton, NJ: Houghton Mifflin, 1974), "Early Critical Comment on the Plays and Poems," 1847. See also Ann Thompson and Sasha Roberts, eds., *Women Reading Shakespeare, 1660-1900: An Anthology of Criticism* (Manchester, UK: Manchester University Press, 2013), 11-14.

[155] About Cavendish's "unusual, grandiloquent format," William Poole notes that she "liked her books to look as imposing as they would sound." Poole, "Margaret Cavendish's Books in New College, and around Oxford," *New College Notes* 6 (2015): 2, http://www.new.ox.ac.uk/ncnotes.

as her translation of Philippe de Mornay's *Discourse of Life and Death*, the play was printed in a quarto volume; when it was published as a separate text in 1595, it was printed in the smaller octavo format. Elizabeth Cary's 1613 *Mariam* was also a quarto volume.

The quarto and octavo formats were the standard for individual plays in early-modern publishing. Even for collections of plays, there were other precedents besides the folio. In 1632, for example, the London publisher Edward Blount produced a collection of plays by John Lyly, *Six Court Comedies*, in a duodecimo volume, the same format William Cavendish chose when he published two plays, *The Country Captain* and *The Variety*, in a single volume in 1649.[156] In 1651, the poet and dramatist William Cartwright published a multi-genre collection, *Comedies, Tragicomedies, with Other Poems*, in an octavo volume, while the Caroline dramatist Richard Brome published two collections of plays, both titled, confusingly, *Five New Plays*, the first in 1653 and the second in 1659, each in octavo format.[157] James Shirley's *Six New Plays* was also published in 1653, in an octavo volume.[158] In 1662, the year Margaret Cavendish published her *Plays*, another collection of plays appeared, in a duodecimo size, the *Gratiae Theatrales*.[159]

However, Cavendish did not choose one of these smaller-sized volumes. When she published her plays, she decided to present them in the large folio format she had used for her earlier publications. This was not a casual or accidental decision. In her analysis of Cavendish's printing choices, Rebecca Bullard observes that "prestigious, folio format creates an impression of monumentality that reflects Cavendish's

---

[156] On the sizes of folios, quartos, and octavos, see above, n. 12. To produce a duodecimo volume, a single sheet of paper is folded into twelve leaves, producing twenty-four pages. William Cavendish's *The Humorous Lover* and *The Triumphant Widow*, published in 1677, were each produced in quarto volumes.

[157] The 1653 *Five New Plays* contained *A Mad Couple Well-Match'd*, *The Novella*, *The Court Beggar*, *The City Wit*, and *The Demoiselle*; the 1659 *Five New Plays* contained *The English Moor*, *The Lovesick Court*, *The Weeding of Covent Garden*, *The New Academy*, and *The Queen and Concubine*.

[158] Shirley's collection contained *The Brothers*, *Sisters*, *The Doubtfull Heir*, *The Imposture*, *The Cardinall*, and *The Court Secret*.

[159] *Gratiae Theatrales, or, a Choice Ternary of English Plays Composed upon Especial Occasions by Several Ingenious Persons* (London, 1662). The volume's plays included *Thorny-Abbey, or The London-maid* "by T. W.," *The marriage-broker, or The pander* "by M. W. M.A.," and *Grim the collier of Croydon, or The devil and his dame* "by I. T."

desire to speak to posterity."[160] The folio is also the format William Cavendish used, not when he published his plays, but for his masterwork on horses and horsemanship, *La Méthode et invention nouvelle de dresser les chevaux*, published in 1658. As Katie Whitaker describes it, this lavish volume "was a luxury item" and one that, with its large-scale format, was not a book William Cavendish could afford to produce himself—he needed financial backers. Margaret Cavendish's decision to collect her *plays* and publish them in a folio volume was guaranteed not only to draw attention to them but also to align her collection with those of Jonson, Shakespeare, and Beaumont and Fletcher.[161] Indeed, it is a comparison she invites as she draws explicit connections between her plays and theirs, at once praising her male predecessors even while suggesting that her plays are, in some sense, *better* than the works of these great literary forefathers.

Jonson's 1616 *Works* established a precedent for the dramatic folios that were to follow: a frontispiece and elaborate title page, a series of commendatory verses addressed to the playwright by fellow poets, then the individual play texts. This arrangement was echoed in the Shakespeare First Folio of 1623, with the addition of a verse written by Ben Jonson himself and addressed "To the Reader" as well as a dedication of the volume to two noble patrons (William Herbert, earl of Pembroke, and his brother Philip Herbert, earl of Montgomery) and an epistle "To the Great Variety of Readers" written by the collection's editors, John Heminge and Philip Condell.[162] Like the 1623 Shakespeare collection, the 1647 Beaumont and Fletcher folio, produced by the publishers Humphrey Robinson and Humphrey Moseley, was published after the two dramatists' deaths—Beaumont had died in 1616, Fletcher in 1625. Following the Jonson and Shakespeare precedents, the folio opened with a portrait, though, oddly of Fletcher alone (in his preface to the reader Moseley comments, "I was very ambitious to have got Mr. Beaumont's picture, but could not possibly, though I spared no inquiry"), the facing title page emphasizing that the plays within the

---

[160] Bullard, "Gatherings in Exile: Interpreting the Bibliographical Structure of *Nature's Pictures Drawn by Fancies Pencil to the Life* (1656)," *English Studies* 92, no. 7 (2011): 803.

[161] See above, 3-5.

[162] William Herbert and his brother were the sons of Mary Sidney Herbert, countess of Pembroke.

volume were "never printed before."[163] Thirty-seven commendatory poems follow, many of them stressing male friendship, not only the bonds between Beaumont and Fletcher but also the bonds of friendship between the various writers of the praise addressed to the two writing partners.[164] The volume also includes a dedicatory epistle from surviving actors of the King's Company addressed to Philip Herbert, now earl of Pembroke (and the sole surviving brother of the Heminge and Condell dedication), and a preface addressed "To the Reader," written by the playwright John Shirley.

In her 1662 *Plays*, Cavendish demonstrates her awareness of all of this—and her anxieties are evident. Even while following, or attempting to follow, what Jeffrey Masten identifies as the "patriarchal model" established by Jonson's 1616 *Works*, Cavendish has to make adjustments.[165] In one respect, of course, she could emulate the model her predecessors offered, not only in the size of her volume but also in the richness and extensiveness of their prefatory materials. At the same time, it is a model with which she struggled: she had no playwriting colleagues to produce commendatory verses addressed to her on the occasion of the folio's publication. Instead of opening her volume with page after page of poems full of praise, she carefully enclosed her fourteen comedies and tragedies within a protective frame, a series of explanations, justifications, defenses, and apologies.

The large folio volume begins with an impressive but contradictory two-page spread.[166] On the left is an engraved frontispiece featuring a

---

[163] Humphrey Moseley, "The Stationer to the Reader," quoted in Masten, *Textual Intercourse*, 123. Masten notes (p. 147) that Moseley had tried to publish the collection earlier, but that the King's Men had "blocked" him from doing so—however, the plays "had lost all utility for them with the closing of the theatres in 1642," making their publication possible.

[164] On this "strange unimitable intercourse," the "unimitated" intimate relationship established between the writers in this volume, see Masten, *Textual Intercourse*, 132-38.

[165] Masten, *Textual Intercourse*, 123.

[166] The dimensions of surviving copies of *Playes* vary, depending on how the pages have been cropped and the books bound. British Library 79.I.14 measures 30.2 cm by 18.5 cm (approximately 11.9 inches by 7.3 inches), with the interior pages measuring 28.2 cm by 17.5 cm (approximately 11.1 inches by 6.9 inches). By comparison (for generations of students who have hauled it around), the dimensions of *The Riverside Shakespeare* are 10.1 inches by 8.2 inches, though at 2.6 inches thick (some 2000 pages), it is twice as thick as Cavendish's volume, which measures 3.3 cm (1.3 inches).

portrait of Cavendish, not a simple bust, as in her predecessors' folios, but a full-length image of the author displayed as a classical sculpture.[167] Her flowing robes conceal much of her figure but not her rounded breasts. Despite the multiple folds of the ermine-lined robe, which she lifts up provocatively, we can see that she is posed *contrapposto*, standing with her weight on her left foot, her right leg bent, her shoulders and torso slightly turned to face forward. This is a pose we find often in Renaissance sculpture—we see it in Michelangelo's *David*, for example, and Cavendish's pose in the classically inspired setting looks almost like a mirror image of that famous work. Her figure is placed within an arched niche and, as if the arch is just a bit too low to accommodate her, the small coronet she is wearing is askew, sliding down the back of her head. She is flanked by two classical gods: on her right is Athena, the virgin-goddess of wisdom and the arts, wearing a helmet and carrying a staff and shield, on which is the head of her disgraced priestess, Medusa; on Cavendish's left is Apollo, god of music and prophecy, holding a lyre and a scepter topped with a rayed sun. The gods ignore Cavendish, however, preferring to stare at each other from their respective pedestals. Cavendish pays them no mind. Instead of gazing serenely away from the viewer, as Michelangelo's David does, Cavendish is looking out of her image on the page and directly at us, inviting, if not welcoming, our gaze.[168]

In the engraving, Cavendish stands on a plinth inscribed with an untitled twelve-line poem, startling in its echo of the verses that open the Shakespeare First Folio. There, however, Jonson's poem is not part of

---

[167] See Figure 1. The frontispiece was engraved by the Flemish engraver Pieter van Schuppen from a design by the Dutch artist Abraham van Diepenbeke, and it was first used several years earlier, in the 1655 *Worlds Olio*. The Cavendish frontispieces (there are three) have intrigued her biographers; Jones, *A Glorious Fame*, includes only one, but Grant reproduces all three in *Margaret the First*, as does Whitaker in *Mad Madge*.

[168] Theodora Jankowski describes Cavendish's pose in this image—"with her right hand on her hip and her elbow pointed toward, and looking over her right shoulder at the viewer"—as a "regal stance," comparing it to Anthony van Dyck's portrait of Charles I "in hunting dress." The English king does not wear a crown, but the painter depicts "Charles with his left hand on his hip, elbow bent and pointed toward the viewer, looking superciliously over his shoulder at his audience." Jankowski believes the pose in the Cavendish frontispiece "was obviously copied by van Scuppen": "Cavendish appears to tread upon sovereign turf here in her chosen pose." Jankowski, "Critiquing the Sexual Economies of Marriage," in *The History of British Women's Writing*, vol. 3, *1610-1690*, ed. Mihoko Suzuki (New York: Palgrave Macmillan, 2911), 234.

the engraved bust of the author but faces the title page, with the opening lines pointing to and commenting on the portrait of Shakespeare: "This figure that thou here seest put / It was for gentle Shakespeare cut." Jonson laments the inability of the engraver to capture the poet's wit as well as his image, the final couplet addressed directly to the reader: "But since he cannot, reader, look / Not on his picture but his book." The verses inscribed on Cavendish's plinth are much the same—but not quite. The author of the verses—who is speaking?—immediately issues us a command, not a gentle invitation to look: "Here on this figure cast a glance." But even as we are ordered to view the image, we are warned not to stare too long or too intently. We should look casually, "as if it were by chance," and then only briefly. Our eyes "must not stay." The figure of Cavendish is meant to be seen but not to be studied. Moreover, we are instructed that "this" representation, though beautiful, is a mere shadow. We will not find Cavendish's true beauty in the artist's portrait, however well it might capture the "lovely lines" of her face and form, but in her writing; only there will we discover "her soul's picture." At the verse's end, we are issued a final order: "read those lines which she hath writ."[169] This ambiguous image, both demanding that we look even as it redirects our attention, faces a title page that is entirely unambiguous. It boldly announces the volume's contents, "PLAYES," and Cavendish's authorship: "written by the thrice noble, illustrious and excellent princess, the Lady Marchioness of Newcastle." While the title of her book is set in large capital letters, her name extends over eight lines of increasingly emphatic type.[170]

---

[169] The notion that the best portrait of the artist is found in his work is also seen in the Beaumont and Fletcher folio, where Humphrey Moseley explains his failure to include a portrait of Beaumont: "the best pictures and those most like him you'll find in this volume." Moseley, "The Stationer to the Reader," quoted in Masten, *Textual Intercourse*, 124.

[170] See Figure 2. In this title, the adverb "thrice" is used as an intensifier, to mean "very" or "extremely" (*OED*).

There is a large printer's device following Cavendish's name. At first glance, it looks rather like a Hershey's chocolate kiss, but the image is an angel standing on one foot on top of a bell; the angel is blowing a trumpet (a puff of air emerges from the trumpet's mouth). A motto swirling around the angel's feet reads "vi veneranda sones." The device and motto seem to refer to judgment day—see, for example, the poet John Andrews, *A Subpoena from the High Imperiall Court of Heaven to Be Served upon All Men* (London, 1620), who counsels his readers to remember always that death is near: "Ever do think thou hearst his trumpet blow / Sure the time is even now at hand." Each

Following this impressive double-page spread is an array of prefatory material, superficially not unlike that in the folio volumes of her male predecessors. Cavendish begins with a six-line verse dedication of her book to "those that do delight in scenes and wit." These brief lines are followed by "The Epistle Dedicatory," although it is not addressed to a noble patron of her work but to her husband, William Cavendish, whom she greets as "my lord." A sequence of nine epistles, each one individually titled "To the Readers," follows. Most of these addresses are relatively brief, just a paragraph in length, but a few are longer, with one extending to two full pages of closely printed prose. There is a tenth such "letter," tacked on and lacking the embellished printer's ornament, large title heading, and salutation that carefully mark out each of the preceding nine. Although printed on its own page, this last seems more like a hastily written postscript than a final dedicatory epistle, beginning, without a preamble, "I must trouble my noble readers to write of one thing more." And yet this "one more thing" is not the last thing we encounter.

Still turning the pages and looking for her plays, we encounter yet another dedication, this one a poem "upon her plays," written by Cavendish's husband. This is the single commendatory poem included in her collection. It is followed by Cavendish's own 104-line "General Prologue to All My Plays" in rhymed couplets. It is here that she draws an explicit link between her work and that of Jonson, Shakespeare, and Beaumont and Fletcher. She begins with a reference to Jonson, though one that immediately warns readers that her plays will *not* be like his: "Noble spectators, do not think to see such plays that's like Ben Jonson's," whose dramas were "masterpieces and were wrought by wit's invention." She follows this praise of Jonson's plays by a lengthy dispraise of her own that are, by contrast, lacking wit, quickly written, and not the result of serious study but of "play" and idleness. By implication, she aligns herself as a writer to "gentle Shakespeare" and his "fluent wit"; he had "less learning" than Jonson, yet his plays, written solely through "nature's light," give his "readers and spectators sight." Having contrasted these two great writers of drama, Cavendish once again excuses her own efforts even while hinting that her work is, in some crucial sense, superior to that of her male predecessors. Unlike

---

sinner's "debt" will be due on Judgment Day, Andrew reminds his readers, and only repentance "keeps you from eternal fire." Following "Finis" appears the same admonitory motto: "Vi veneranda sones."

them, Cavendish makes it clear that she does *not* "steal" her language, plots, and themes from any sources:

> But, noble readers, do not think my plays
> Are such as have been writ in former days,
> As Jonson, Shakespeare, Beaumont, Fletcher writ—
> Mine want their learning, reading, language, wit,
> The Latin phrases I could never tell,
> But Jonson could, which made him write so well;
> Greek, Latin poets, I could never read,
> Nor their historians, but our English speed,
> I could not steal their wit, nor plots out take,
> All my plays' plots my own brain did make.

Unlike the plays of Jonson, Shakespeare, and Beaumont and Fletcher, her work is *entirely* her own: "All the materials in my head did grow, / All is my own, and nothing do I owe."[171]

After this prologue, we turn the page to discover "An Introduction," written in the form of a dramatic scene.[172] The two-page play opens, immediately, without any setting or stage direction other than "Enter three gentlemen." One of these gentlemen abruptly confronts his companion. "Come, Tom," he asks, "will you go to a play?" Tom's answer is simple and direct: "No." But this clear response doesn't satisfy the first gentleman. When pressed about why he won't go, Tom again replies simply and directly: "Because there is so many words and so little wit, as the words tire me more than the wit delights me." And besides, he adds, the actors are bad, as are the plays in which they appear. Neither Tom nor the third gentleman, who does not seem much of a fan of plays himself, is convinced by the first gentleman's eagerness, and as the scene progresses, Tom is compelled to reiterate the reasons for his refusal: plays are full of "empty words, dull speeches, long parts, tedious acts, ill

---

[171] Cavendish, "A General Prologue," *Playes*, A7r-AA7r. I have silently modernized the spelling and punctuation. Cavendish embeds a similar critique in the text of *The Female Academy*, 4.22.

[172] Cavendish, "An Introduction," *Playes*, 1-2. I have silently modernized the spelling and punctuation. Interestingly, like the rest of the plays in the volume, the pages of "An Introduction" are numbered, and the play that follows immediately, *Loves Adventures*, begins on p. 3.

actors." As if that isn't enough, he adds that "there is not enough variety in old plays" to please him.

Only at this point does the first and most enthusiastic gentleman tell his companions that he wants them to go with him to see a *new* play—even more surprising, this new play is written by a woman. Tom is shocked: "A woman write a play! Out upon it, out upon it, for it cannot be good. Besides, you say she is a lady, which is the likelier to make the play worse. A woman and a lady to write a play? Fie, fie." After further debate about whether a woman can write a play at all, much less a good one—accompanied by the worry that, if a woman *were* to write a good play, it would mean that men would lose their "preeminence"—Tom grudgingly agrees to go along with his companions, although it's not clear whether he has finally been convinced to give the female-authored play a chance or whether he decides to go simply because he doesn't want to be left behind. In the end, Tom will only say that he is "contented to cast away so much time for the sake of the sex" despite the fact that he has "no faith" in the "authoress's wit." But "Who knows?" asks the third gentleman in the last line of this "Introduction," at the very bottom of page. Since many sinners convert and repent after hearing a "good sermon," Tom might change his mind after "seeing this play." On the next page, *Love's Adventure*, subtitled *Play*, begins.

The question of whether Tom changes his mind about the play written by a "lady" remains unanswered. As the readers to whom Cavendish's many epistles are addressed, we might regard the fourteen comedies and tragedies in *Plays* as the definitive proof of a woman's ability to write a good play or, more specifically, of the marchioness of Newcastle's ability to do so.[173] But, while "An Introduction" is a witty dramatization of the anxieties of authorship that are revealed throughout the prefatory materials in the 1662 *Plays*, there is no return to this group of three gentlemen at the end of the volume, no response to "An Introduction" in a final scene titled "A Conclusion," a little play at the end of the collection showing Tom's conversion and repentance.

---

[173] It is somewhat difficult to number Cavendish's plays in this volume. Today the contents are usually tallied at fourteen, but six of the plays are in two parts. If these were counted separately, the number of plays in the collection would number twenty. In the letter to her readers at the end of *Playes*, however, Cavendish says she's completed twenty-one plays.

Instead, Cavendish completes the frame around her plays with one more letter addressed to her "noble readers."

In this final epistle, Cavendish apologizes if some of us have had more than "enough" of her plays "to cloy" our "gusto." Perhaps the plays haven't "whet" our "appetites" but have instead managed to make us a little sick to our stomachs. Considering this possibility, Cavendish suggests that maybe we should just read *one* of the plays she has written (interesting advice, here at the end of the collection), and if this one play proves to be "unpleasant or hard of digestion," then we needn't bother to read any more. We may not enjoy the taste of her "poetical dishes"; she is, after all, just a "plain" English cook who can't produce fancy delicacies to tempt the appetites of those of us who might prefer rich dishes. "You may turn me away, which is to put my works out of your studies," she writes, adding, "I only desire I may not depart with your displeasures, but as an honest, poor servant that rather wanted art and skill in my works than will or endeavor to make or dress them to every palate." In any case, she is still hard at work writing, with more to come soon. She acknowledges having promised her readers that she "would not trouble" them with "any more" of her works even as she offers a preview of her next project.[174] Then, after nearly seven hundred pages, she is done: "And so farewell."[175]

Rather than acting as a welcome to the readers she addresses so fulsomely in *Plays*, all of this—the initial dedication, the long series of letters, William Cavendish's praise of his wife and her work, the prologue, the introduction, and the farewell address—seems instead to pose a challenge, if not an obstacle, to her readers. Cavendish protects her plays behind a wall of words. She erects a formidable, almost impenetrable, barrier of complaints and apologies, self-praise and self-criticism, modesty and boastfulness, at once normalizing her act of playwriting even while proclaiming her unique status as a writer of plays.

---

[174] Cavendish indicates that she's already completed "above threescore letters" and hopes "to make them up a hundred; Cavendish exceeded her goals, publishing *CCXI Sociable Letters, Written by the Thrice Noble, Illustrious, and Excellent Princess, the Lady Marchioness of Newcastle* in 1664.

[175] Cavendish's final epistle follows *The Female Academy*, in *Playes*, 653-79.

Figure 1.

Frontispiece, *Playes* (1662)

Used by Permission of the National Portrait Gallery (London)

Figure 2.

Title page, *Playes* (1662)

Margaret Cavendish's *The Female Academy* (1662)

In taking up the subject of women's education in *The Female Academy*, Margaret Cavendish is returning to a subject she has previously addressed, not only in dedicatory epistles prefacing her published works but also in "Of Gentlewomen That Are Sent to Board Schools," an essay included in *The World's Olio*.[176] While Cavendish may be a strong advocate *of* educating women, she is not an advocate of educational institutions *for* women—or at least for the kind of boarding schools that had become very popular in Restoration London.[177] Cavendish thinks the educational programs found in such schools are not only superficial but harmful, perhaps because, as one modern historian has observed, the mission of such schools was often "to transform the daughters of the merchant class into young ladies suitable for marriage to gentry," the curriculum designed primarily to instruct students in good grooming, proper demeanor, and appropriate female arts, like singing, dancing, and needlework.[178]

"It is dangerous to put young women to board schools," Cavendish cautions her readers, unless the situation is dire—unless, for example,

---

[176] Cavendish addresses the state of women's education in epistles prefacing both *The Philosophical and Physical Opinions* and *The Worlds Olio*, see above, 18-20.

[177] For an introduction to the subject of girls' boarding schools in seventeenth-century England, see Martine Sonnet, "A Daughter to Educate," trans. Arthur Goldhammer, in *A History of Women in the West*, vol. 3, *Renaissance and Enlightenment Paradoxes*, ed. Natalie Zemon Davis and Arlette Farge (Cambridge: Harvard University Press), 116-17. According to Sonnet, the first boarding school for young women in London opened in 1617, and by the middle of the century, "any city worthy of the name boasted a boarding school" (116). As many as fourteen such schools for girls were operating in London during this period, especially in the suburbs of Chelsea, Hackney, and Putney.

In 1649, Sir John Evelyn (above, 27) records in his diary that he "went to Putney by water, in the barge with diverse ladies, to see the schools or colleges of the learned gentlewomen" (17 June 1649, in *The Diary and Correspondence of Sir John Evelyn*, ed. Bray, 1:259). At the same time, in Hackney, one boarding school for girls was such a "sought-after institution" that it became known as the "ladies' university of the female arts." In April 1667, Samuel Pepys (see above, 26-27) attended Hackney Church in large part to see the schoolgirls: "That which we went chiefly to see was the young ladies of the schools, whereof there is great store, very pretty" (Samuel Pepys, 21 April 1667, in *The Diary of Samuel Pepys . . .* , ed. Henry B. Wheatley, 6:179.)

[178] Sonnet, "A Daughter to Educate," *Renaissance and Enlightenment Paradoxes*, 116. By the end of the century, Sonnet also notes, "these institutions were being widely criticized for dispensing a superficial education" (116).

"their parents live so disorderly as their children may grow wicked or base by their examples."[179] In such schools, young women "learn more vices than good manners": they "may educate their persons, but it is a doubt whether they do, or can, educate their minds." Schools "may learn them to sing well, but it is a question whether they learn them to think well, they may learn them measures with the feet and mistake the measures of a good life, they may learn them to write by rule but forget the rules of modesty." Nor is there safety in numbers—while young women might be educated well if they are taught "singly, carefully, and industriously, one by one," there is only trouble when "a great many women" of "different dispositions, natures, and qualities" are "gathered and heaped together" in boarding schools. Together they learn not as much from their teachers as from one another, and what they learn is not good: "crafts [cunning], dissembling fraud, spite, slander, or the like."[180] These vices, "like maggots," may "consume their estates" and "eat a hole through their reputation."

But that is not all. What these schools really do for their "scholars of the effeminate sex" is prepare them for consumption, like badly dressed meat for sale "at a cook's shop, which always tastes of the dripping pan or smoke."[181] Just so, those who "are bred at schools have a smack of the school" about them, a sense of "constraint" imposed on them by their schoolmistresses to compel them to proper behavior. But the "noble principles" of "right understanding," virtue, reason, and temperance cannot be learned and exercised under constraint, and they cannot be taught by just anyone, but only by "those that have been nobly bred themselves."[182]

In *The Female Academy*, the final play in her 1662 collection, Cavendish turns her attention to the topic of female education and to the more vexed question of what kind of institution might be appropriate for educating young women. Unlike other plays in the volume, *The Comedy Named the Several Wits*, for example, or *The Comical Hash*, and the first part of *Matrimonial Trouble,* described as *A Comedy*, and the second part as, *A Comedytragedy*, the genre of *The Female Academy* is not specified, nor do the stage directions set the scene. Is this play set in contemporary London or a fanciful, imagined environment? (Wherever this play is set,

---

[179] "Of Gentlewomen That Are Sent to Board Schools," *The World's Olio*, 61.
[180] "Of Gentlewomen That Are Sent to Board Schools," *The World's Olio*, 62.
[181] A *cook's shop* is "shop where cooked food is sold; an eating-house" (*OED*).
[182] "Of Gentlewomen That Are Sent to Board Schools," *The World's Olio*, 62.

it still represents a kind of fantasyland—in contrast to early-modern drama by male playwrights, her play includes an impressive number of female characters who speak far more lines than the male characters.)

Instead of establishing time and place, *The Female Academy* opens quickly with a *fait accompli*—two ladies announce the establishment of an institution devoted exclusively to the education of young women. But this is clearly no boarding house serving up young women as badly cooked beef—the Female Academy is described as "a house wherein a company of young ladies are instructed by old matrons . . . to speak wittily and rationally, . . . to behave themselves handsomely, and to live virtuously." The Academy is also an exclusive place—not only because it excludes all men but because the pupils themselves must be young women of "honorable birth." Without some claim to "ancient descent," an aspiring student will not be admitted—although the reason for the Academy's exclusivity seems less that education is possible only for the well-born than because it costs money to enter. The Academy "is a place of charges."

In this play, Cavendish presents the Female Academy as an institution created by women for women, and by restricting its students to young women of quality, it seems to be designed to avoid many of the problems Cavendish noted in her earlier criticisms of all-female boarding schools. After the first scene, which takes place outside the school, we move inside, where we see the young students in a lecture hall. One of the founding "grave" matrons of the school introduces a female lecturer, who takes the chair and addresses her fellow students, described in Cavendish's stage directions as "a company of young ladies." The play also allows us to see the reactions of men, excluded from the Female Academy. Instead of ignoring the school, or wishing its young pupils well in their educational pursuits, men can't stay away—they hang around and spy on what's going on through "a large open grate" that allows them to hear the lectures being given inside. Although women have moved into the secure space of the Female Academy, this open grate maintains a link between the young women inside the Female Academy and the men in the outside world.

Indeed, the rest of this play alternates between scenes focusing on the educational accomplishments of the women *inside* the Female Academy and scenes showing the increasing agitation of the men *outside* the school. The women's "discourses" are neither frivolous in subject nor ridiculous in delivery; over the course of the play, the speakers address themselves at some length to serious intellectual topics, not to perfecting dance steps or embroidery skills. The pattern of instruction is always the same. One of the matrons introduces the "theme" of the lecture, which is then presented by a "lady speaker." The students' lectures include topics like "whether women are capable to have as much wit or wisdom as men," two long disquisitions on logic and rhetoric, an explication of "the behavior of women," an exploration of truth, a discussion of language, a discourse on friendship, another on a survey of literature and literary genres, and an extended discussion of vanity, vice, and wickedness. The scenes inside the Female Academy are static—each is really an extended monologue delivered by the various "lady speakers" addressing themselves to a quiet and attentive group of students.[183] As far as we can see, the women inside the school spend all of their time educating themselves on these sober topics and no time fooling around with fraud, spite, and slander.

The scenes outside the Female Academy are, by contrast, frantic. Angry that the women "should speak so much" and themselves "so little," the "young gentlemen" decide to set up a rival academy right next to the Female Academy—they appropriate the room where they had watched the female speakers through the Academy's grate and set up their own school in that very spot so that "the ladies may hear what they can say." But rather than demonstrating their superiority, the men begin by "rail[ing] extremely" that so many "fair young ladies are so strictly enclosed as not to suffer men to visit them in the Academy." In fact, a later scene makes it clear that the young men have no other topic on their mind, "for," as one gentleman speaker admits, "our minds are so full of thoughts of the female sex we have no room for any other subject or object." Without women, men can only think about them, talk about them, and complain about how "ungrateful" they are. None of the women inside the Academy makes use of the grate to listen in on the men's lectures.

One gentleman speaker who takes the chair to give the longest lecture in the men's school delivers a speech all about men's superiority to

---

[183] Cavendish is familiar with the kinds of brief prose disquisitions she writes for her lady speakers. There are many short explorations of the kinds of topics her speakers address in *The Female Academy* in *Philosophicall fancies* (1653), *The Worlds Olio* (1655), and especially in *Orations of Divers Sorts*, published in 1662, the same year as *Playes*. And a similar series of lectures is presented by a woman speaker in the two-part *Natures Three Daughters, Beauty, Love, and Wit* (*Playes*, 489-527); on similarities between the "discourses" in these two plays, see below, *The Female Academy*, 1.2. (n. 11).

women, arguing men's superior strength, their manifold accomplishments, their greater knowledge, and their proper role as instructors for women. Actually, this long, angry rant sounds suspiciously like Cavendish's own defense of male superiority in her preface to *The World's Olio*—and it almost seems as if she has reconsidered what she wrote about male superiority in the 1650s and has now recycled her own words, putting them into the mouth of a ridiculous young man. In this context, the speaker's claim to male superiority is wickedly satirized, since his claims that women can't be educated by other women and that they are unable to comprehend serious subjects are belied by the educational program of the Female Academy. Two scenes later, we see what men's claims to superiority really mean, at least from the perspective of another angry young man: women have become "so self-conceited" that they "usurp . . . masculine power and authority, and instead of being dutiful, humble, and obedient to men, as they ought to be, they are tyrannical tyrannizers."

The men are forced to admit that their lectures aren't coming off very well when compared to those of their female rivals. One gentleman admits that "the men's discourses are simple, childish, and foolish in comparison [to] the women's." His disgruntled companion agrees, but argues that since their lectures are about women, who are simple, foolish, and childish, any discussion of women must, of necessity, be simple, foolish, and childish. Even worse, the men eventually realize that, no matter how far-ranging the women's curriculum, there is one subject that is of no interest to them at all: "they neither mention the men nor their discourse nor [their] arguments nor [their] academy, as if there were no such thing as men." The young men conclude that their situation is grim—because "all the youngest, fairest, richest, and noblest ladies" have enrolled in the Female Academy, there are only old women left outside. And if all the desirable young women have "encloistered themselves," then "it is a dangerous example for all the rest of their sex." By educating themselves, then, women are threatening not just the established social order but the very survival of the species: if all the eligible young women choose to enroll in the Female Academy, "there would be none left out to breed on."

This last is a subtle reminder of the exclusive nature of the Female Academy, a point that is emphasized in an earlier scene where two "citizen wives" are on their way to hear one of the female speakers. They return quickly, having been "beat back" by a "doorkeeper" who tells them that there is "no room for citizen wives, for the room was only kept for ladies and gentlewomen of quality." In *The Female Academy*, Cavendish suggests that education is not for every woman; it is equally clear that the daughters of "citizen wives" are no fit mates for the play's desperate young gentlemen—who aren't desperate enough to consider them as eligible "to breed on." Nevertheless, no matter how unsuitable they might be as wives, the angry men fear that young women who are not eligible for admission to the Academy will be led astray by the example of the elite young ladies enrolled in the Female Academy.

In the end, however—just at the last moment, in the very last few lines of the last scene—Cavendish's play takes an unexpected turn. The matron of the Female Academy leaves the school to tell the anxious and frustrated young men that they "are in great error." Her students haven't "vowed virginity," nor have they "encloistered" themselves, for the Academy is not a convent but "a school wherein [her pupils] are taught how to be good wives when they are married." The matron claims that young women have been instructed in "duty and obedience," but how and when the pupils may have received their lessons in duty and obedience isn't at all clear to us because we haven't observed any such kind of instruction. If the young women have been lectured on these topics, these aren't the lectures the playwright has chosen to write. The matron encourages the young men to hurry off to her pupils' friends and families to make arrangements for securing the properly educated—that is, the dutiful and obedient—young women as wives. In the last line of the play, the gentlemen thank the matron: "we shall be your servants, for your favors." According to Cavendish's final stage direction, they "go out," with the gentlemen "waiting on" the matron, "with their hats in their hands, scraping" and "congying" (bowing low in respect) to her.

What are we to make of this sudden turn of events? Is *The Female Academy*, after all, yet another Cavendish commentary on the uselessness of female boarding schools? Or does the play make a sober and disheartening statement about the limits of female agency—the young women are put in the school by their mothers, apparently without any say about it, only to be turned over (purportedly, at any rate) as wives to young men, equally without consultation. Is the play thus to be read as a tragedy, one where young women who have the time and freedom to engage in intellectual pursuits are suddenly returned to the constraints imposed on their sex? Where innocent girls are unwittingly prepared for marriage and served up to young men by a knowing and experienced female accomplice?

Or is *The Female Academy* a comedy—one in which young women who have been forced into a dreary educational institution suddenly and happily find themselves restored to glorious liberty? What could be more humorous than an educated woman? What resolution could be happier than to become a wife to such ill-qualified and unattractive young men? What could be more surprising than a sober matron who reveals herself to be a practiced bawd? "I will endeavor to serve you," the matron informs the importunate young men, "and shall be proud of the employment that you shall be pleased to impose to my trust and management."

Or is the conclusion of the play not at all what it seems to be at first reading. Rather than betraying the young women inside the Female Academy, does the matron trick the gentlemen causing so much disturbance outside the academy by sending them off on a futile mission not only to seek the "good liking and assent" of the young ladies' parents but also to earn the "good liking" of their would-be brides. "If you be worthy gentlemen, as I believe you all are," the matron tells them, "their love will be due to your merits, and your merits will persuade them to love you." These young men have certainly not demonstrated any particular worthiness throughout the play, nor do their "merits" seem likely to earn them the love of any reasonable—and now reasonably educated—young woman. Is the matron's action a clever ruse rather than an unexpected reversal or an uncomfortable betrayal?

Is Cavendish's *The Female Academy* just one more early-modern play mocking women's educational aspirations? Not all sixteenth- and early seventeenth-century playwrights made fun of educated women, of course—in fact, Cavendish's idol, Shakespeare, made gentle fun not of women who devote themselves to learning but of a group of young men who decide to dedicate themselves for three years' time to an all-male "little academe."[184] In *Love's Labour's Lost*, these young friends swear not only to spend their time fasting and studying but also to avoiding the company of women. Berowne, one of the "young lords" who makes up this dedicated group, is fearful that "Nature will make us all forsworn / Three thousand times within this three years / space."[185] Nevertheless,

---

[184] William Shakespeare, *Love's Labour's Lost*, in *The Riverside Shakespeare*, ed. G. Blakemore Evans (New York: Houghton Mifflin, 1974), 1.1.13.

[185] *Love's Labour's Lost*, 1.1.149-50.

he signs his name to the "strict decrees" even while acknowledging their folly: "I'll lay my head to any good man's hat, / These oaths and laws will prove an idle scorn."[186] But, while Shakespeare took aim at the pretensions of the young men and their "male academy," the fun was usually at women's expense in the plays of his contemporaries— although men enjoyed exclusive access to educational institutions, early-modern playwrights were quick to turn their "idle scorn" on female characters who tried to create such spaces for themselves.

One of the most brutal examples is to be found in Ben Jonson's *Epicoene, or the Silent Woman*, first acted in 1609 and subsequently published in his 1616 collected works.[187] Among the many targets of Jonson's misogyny in this play is a "new foundation . . . in the town, of ladies, that call themselves the collegiates." These "collegiate ladies" represent a threat to the social order; they dare to live apart from their husbands, dare to "give entertainment to all the wits and braveries [fashionably dressed young gallants] of the time," and dare to express their own views. Their worst crime, in fact, seems to be that they have opinions: they "cry down, or up, what they like or dislike in a brain or a fashion with most masculine, or rather hermaphroditical, authority." And to compound the danger, "every day" they try to find and admit some "new probationer" to their "college."[188] When Jonson shows us the "collegiate ladies" in school, at their lessons, we quickly discover that their "college-grammar" consists mainly in learning how to plaster themselves with make-up in order to "repair the losses time and years have made in their features" and how to lure unsuspecting men into their clutches.[189] Cavendish no doubt knew Jonson's comedy—her husband had been one of Jonson's longtime patrons, and William Cavendish seems to have provided most of Jonson's financial support in the years before the playwright's death 1637. And as we have already noted, Margaret Cavendish shows her familiarity with Jonson's work in the preface to her 1662 collection of plays, where she refers specifically to *Volpone* and *The Alchemist* when she is defending the length of her own dramatic efforts.

---

[186] *Love's Labour's Lost*, 1.1.308-9.

[187] Ben Jonson, *Epicoene, or the Silent Woman*, in *Works* (1616; rpt. London, 1640), 460-522.

[188] *Epicoene*, 1.1. I have silently modernized the spelling and punctuation.

[189] *Epicoene*, 4.1. I have silently modernized the spelling and punctuation.

While in exile with her husband in Europe, Cavendish might also have come to know Molière's *Les présieuses ridicules* (*The Pretentious Young Ladies*), the French dramatist's 1659 satire of two young provincial women's aspirations to improve themselves in Paris—they dare to want a better life, they yawn at the conversation of young men, they presume to write poetry and plays, they have opinions about actors and dancers, they long for romance and adventure, and so they must be humiliated for their "impertinence," "affectation," and "fooleries."[190] Margaret Cavendish did not read French—but since her husband translated Molière's *L'Étourdi, ou le contretemps* [*The Bungler*] into English, he almost certainly shared the French playwright's popular contemporary works with his wife.[191] Molière may even have had the duchess herself at least partly in mind in his 1672 play, *Les femmes savant* (*The Learned Ladies*)— like Margaret Cavendish, Philaminte writes poems, has a telescope, and takes up the study of science and philosophy. She also plans her own Academy: "women may be learned if they please," she insists, "And found, like men, their own academies."[192] She's got a curriculum for this female academy as well: "Ours, furthermore, shall be more wisely run / Than theirs: we'll roll all disciplines into one, / Uniting letters, in a rich alliance, / With all the tools and theories of science. . . ."[193]

More important than these other playwrights, though, William Cavendish wrote his own play satirizing female pretensions to education, *The Variety*, performed by the King's Men in 1641 and published in 1649.[194] We know Cavendish was influenced by her husband's plays—as she reminds him in the "Epistle Dedicatory" of her 1662 collection, "I believe I should never have writ [these plays], nor have had the capacity nor ingenuity to have writ plays, had not you read to me some plays which your lordship had writ. . . ." What must she have made of *The Variety*—which, like Jonson's *Epicoene*, satirizes "educated women" in the person of Mistress Voluble, whose "academy" includes a curriculum

---

[190] Molière, *The Pretentious Young Ladies*, trans. Henri van Laun, *The Dramatic Works of Molière* (1875; rev. ed. Philadelphia: George Barrie, [n.d.]), 1:143-67.

[191] William Cavendish's translation of Molierè's play was used by John Dryden for his comedy *Sir Martin Mar-all*, although the play's authorship was originally attributed to William Cavendish. On this see above, 51.

[192] *Molière's The Learned Ladies in a New English Verse Translation*, trans. Richard Wilbur (New York: Dramatists Play Service, 1977), 3.2.

[193] *The Learned Ladies*, trans. Wilbur, 3.2.

[194] *The country captaine and the Varietie, two comedies written by a person of honor* (London, 1649).

for her pupils to be "edified" and "ladyfied."[195] In the second act of *The Variety*, the stage is set with a table and chairs, and a group of women gather to hear Mistress Voluble deliver a lecture. She describes herself as "weak and unworthy" of addressing the women, claiming she is more "deserving to be in the number of disciples than a professor in any of the female sciences." Her long lecture is mainly about ribbons, lace, scented gloves, "and such other correspond things as may be of moment and great consequence" to her avid pupils.[196]

Whatever differences the men in William Cavendish's play have with each other, they are united in their opposition to the women's efforts to educate themselves. "But these ladies are very tedious," one observes, adding, "we must have this lecture put down." "They are more like to purchase Gresham College and enlarge it for public professors," another exclaims. Even more outrageous, "you may live to see another university built and only women commence doctors."[197] A sure way to discredit an educated woman is to raise suspicions about her character, and the men have no compunction about spreading a little salacious gossip. Mistress Voluble may be a fortuneteller or a witch, "guilty of the black art." And not only is she "believed" to be a "devilish cunning woman," Mistress Voluble has had two husbands![198]

In the end, though, her tuition proves its value, at least for one woman whom she assures that "'tis never too late to learn to be a lady."[199] Mistress Voluble manages to "discipline" the Widow Simpleton, a "raw" countrywoman, well enough that she can be passed off as an appropriate wife for a knight, much to her son's satisfaction. No matter how ridiculous the curriculum of Mistress Voluble may be, it still proves to be threatening and dangerous to men—men may be superior to women, but they can still be tricked by them.

But all this still leaves us with no real idea of what to make of Margaret Cavendish's play about women's education and educated women. Up until the very last scene of *The Female Academy*, Cavendish seems to be making a strong argument for women's superiority (or at least for the superiority of women of a certain class), for their aptitude for education, for their ability to teach and learn from one another, for their self-

---

[195] *The Varietie*, 1.1. I have silently modernized the spelling and punctuation.
[196] *The Varietie*, 2.1. I have silently modernized the spelling and punctuation.
[197] *The Varietie*, 2.1. I have silently modernized the spelling and punctuation.
[198] *The Varietie*, 2.1. I have silently modernized the spelling and punctuation.
[199] *The Varietie*, 2.1. I have silently modernized the spelling and punctuation.

sufficiency and their disregard for men. Throughout most of the play, it certainly seems as if Cavendish has changed her mind about all-female schools and is writing back vehemently not only to her own earlier position but also to male playwrights who made a mockery of women's pretensions to academic pursuits, including her own husband. *The Female Academy* is even positioned as the last play in Cavendish's collection— it's almost as if, by placing it at the very end of her own dramatic productions, she intends to have the last word on the subject. But what, exactly, does she mean by that last word?

The Legacy of Margaret Cavendish and Her Work

By the time Margaret Cavendish's *Plays* was published in 1662, an Englishwoman had acted for the first time on the public stage in a London playhouse.[200] And a play written by an Englishwoman—or, at least, translated by an Englishwoman—would soon be performed in a public theater. In February of 1663, Katherine Philips's *Pompey*, a translation of the French playwright Pierre Corneille's 1643 tragedy *La Mort de Pompée*, was performed at the Theatre Royal in Dublin; by summer, the play was staged in a London production. Following this success, Philips began translating another of Corneille's tragedies, *Horace*, but she died before she could finish the project. Her translation was completed by John Denham and performed at court in 1668, the same year that Cavendish published her second collection of dramatic work, *Plays, Never before Printed*. In 1669, Philips's *Horace* was staged in London at the Theatre Royal.[201] Later that same year, Frances Boothby's

---

[200] The first recorded performance of an Englishwoman on the public stage in London is generally acknowledged to have occurred on 8 December 1660, when either Margaret Hughes or Anne Marshall (historians differ) performed the role of Desdemona in a production of *Othello* staged by Thomas Killigrew's newly formed King's Company. However, Randall, *Winter Fruit*, argues that Catherine Coleman's performance in the 1656 production of *The Siege of Rhodes* should be recognized as "the first appearance of an actress on a public stage in England" (171). For Coleman, see above, 38-39.

[201] Interestingly, when Katherine Philips's *Pompey* was printed (London, 1663), it appeared in quarto. When a collection of her work was published in 1669, two years after Philips's death and a year after Cavendish's *Plays, Never before Printed*, it was published in a folio format, though one that was not exclusively a collection of plays: *Poems . . . , to which is added . . . Corneille's "Pompey" and "Horace," tragedies. With several other translations out of French* (London, 1669).

tragicomedy, *Marcelina, or The Treacherous Friend*, was performed by the King's Company. It was the first original play by an Englishwoman produced on the English stage. By 1670, Aphra Behn's first play was staged by the Duke's Company, and by the end of the seventeenth century, Elizabeth Polwhele, "Ephelia," "Ariadne," Catherine Trotter, Delariviere Manley, Mary Pix, and Susan Centlivre were all writing for the public theaters.

Whatever inspiration Margaret Cavendish's two collections of plays might have offered for the female dramatists who emerged in the late 1660s, her reputation as a writer was ambiguous. As we have seen, her behavior and clothing received a great deal of public attention when she was in London—her writing, less so. One of the most frequently cited critical assessments of Cavendish's work is Dorothy Osborne's rather horrified comment, preserved in the letters she wrote to the man who would become her husband, Sir William Temple. Their correspondence was a clandestine one; both families opposed the match, and the letters date to the last two years of their separation. Osborne was interested in literature, and her letters frequently referred to what she was reading, for example Madeleine de Scudéry's wildly popular *Artamène, ou le Grand Cyrus* (ten volumes, published between 1648 and 1653) and the heroic romance *Cléopâtre*, by Gauthier de Costes, seigneur de la Calprenède (published in 1648), both of which Osborne read in French. Osborne also mentions "Reine Marguerite," a volume Temple had sent to her and that she returned to him, probably an edition of Marguerite of Navarre's *Memoirs*, published posthumously in 1628. Early in May 1653, writing to Temple in London, Osborne asks if he has "seen a book of poems newly come out by my Lady Newcastle." "For God's sake, if you meet with it, send it me," she exclaims, adding, "they say 'tis ten times more extravagant than her dress." And then, not having read Cavendish's poems, Osborne concludes, "Sure the poor woman is a little distracted; she could never be so ridiculous else as to venture at writing books, and in verse too. If I should not sleep this fortnight, I should not come to that."[202]

Within a few weeks, Osborne had satisfied her curiosity. "You need not send me my Lady Newcastle's book at all," she writes to Temple,

---

[202] Dorothy Osborne to Sir William Temple, 1(?) May 1653, *The Letters of Dorothy Osborne to Sir William Temple*, ed. Edward A. Parry (New York: E. P. Dutton, 1914), 81-82. I have silently modernized the spelling and punctuation.

"for I have seen it, and am satisfied that there are many soberer people in Bedlam. I'll swear her friends are much to blame to let her go abroad."[203] Virginia Woolf used Osborne's initial reaction to Cavendish's "book of poems" as a way to illustrate her claim that "the crazy Duchess became a bogey to frighten clever girls with."[204] Woolf may very well be right in saying that Cavendish and her reputation could be used to scare ambitious young women, but as Osborne's letter makes clear, her opinions had been formed before she had read a single word of *Poems and Fancies*—she was asking Temple to send her a copy when she wrote. Once Evelyn did "see" Cavendish's book, she did not alter her initial view of Cavendish, but it is important to remember that Osborne's views were expressed in her private correspondence, not publicly offered.

In the same way, when Mary Evelyn judges Margaret Cavendish's conversation to be "as airy, empty, whimsical, and rambling as her books," it is not at all clear that she had actually read any of these books. Evelyn also reports, with more than a little skepticism, on the opinions of some of those who *had* been sent copies of Cavendish's work and who vied with one another to praise her during a social gathering. Evelyn claims to have overheard the physician and natural philosopher Walter Charleton "complimenting [Cavendish's] wit and learning in a high manner." For her part, Cavendish does not seem to have taken Charleton's compliments too seriously, since Evelyn reports that the duchess "swore if the schools did not banish Aristotle and read Margaret, duchess of Newcastle, they did her wrong and deserved to be abolished." Evelyn, however, seems to think Cavendish accepted Charleton's excessive praise at face value, receiving it as "so much her due." Evelyn adds that when "a new admirer" approached Cavendish at the gathering, she rewarded him with her views of her faith and religion and even began to "cite her own pieces, line and page in such a book." "I hope," Evelyn concludes in her letter, "as she is an original, she may never have a copy."[205]

---

[203] Dorothy Osborne to Sir William Temple, 12 June (?) 1653, *Letters of Dorothy Osborne*, ed. Parry, 100.

[204] Woolf, *A Room of One's Own*, 62.

[205] Mary Evelyn to the Rev. Ralph Bohun, undated letter from 1667, in *The Diary and Correspondence of John Evelyn*, ed. Bray, 4:8-9. I have silently modernized the spelling and punctuation.

Even if Margaret Cavendish were serious in her comments that her work should replace Aristotle's as a subject of study, Mary Evelyn's prejudices about Cavendish's aspirations are clear, revealed in a letter sent to the same correspondent several years later: "Women were not born to read authors and censure the learned, to compare lives and judge of virtues, to give rules of morality and sacrifice to the muses." Further, "all time borrowed from family duties is misspent. The care of children's education, observing a husband's commands, assisting the sick, relieving the poor, and being serviceable to our friends are of sufficient weight to employ the most improved capacities among us." And then one further damning observation: "if sometimes it happens by accident that one of a thousand aspires a little higher, her fate commonly exposes her to wonder but adds little of esteem."[206] Again, however, it is important to note that, while Mary Evelyn's views on Cavendish and her work are frequently cited by modern critics and biographers, her opinions were, like Dorothy Osborne's, privately shared in personal letters.

Clearly with the aim of a gaining a readership for her work, Margaret Cavendish sent copies of her publications to friends and intellectuals, among them the diplomat and philosopher Sir Kenelm Digby; the renowned philosopher Thomas Hobbes, her husband's friend, to whom she claimed to have "spoken" only a few words; the Cambridge philosopher Henry More; Walter Charleton, the man whom Mary Evelyn overheard complimenting Cavendish on her "wit and learning"; and the playwright Thomas Shadwell. In 1657, Digby wrote to express his appreciation to Cavendish for the "worthy present" of books she had sent, a gift that had inspired in him "new admiration of your goodness and knowledge." But perhaps the praise is a little equivocal—he notes that "every page" in her "excellent book" affords "abundant matter," but that doesn't seem to be saying much.[207] Writing a few years later, in a letter from 1661, Hobbes was a bit more specific, probably having received a copy of *Nature's Pictures*. He tells Cavendish, "I have already read so much of it . . . as to give your excellence an account of it thus

---

[206] Mary Evelyn to the Rev. Ralph Bohun, 4 January 1672, in *The Diary and Correspondence of John Evelyn*, ed. Bray, 4:31-32. I have silently modernized the spelling and punctuation.

[207] Kenelm Digby to Margaret Cavendish, 9 June 1657, in *Letters and Poems*, ed. William Cavendish, 65. I have silently modernized the spelling and punctuation.

far"; her book is "filled throughout with more and truer ideas of virtue and honor than any book of morality I have read."[208]

Henry More dispatched a note to Cavendish expressing his surprise that "so illustrious a person" would send him such "noble volumes as an intended testimony" of her respect—he thought at first the books must have been sent as a gift to his college library, he says, but the duchess's "messenger" insisted they were for him personally. He wrote in haste to thank her before he has had time to "compute the value" of her "most elegant and ingenious writings." But at the same time he was writing to thank Cavendish for her gift, he was privately mocking her philosophical pretensions. In a letter to his friend Anne Finch Conway, whose philosophical education he had nurtured, More belittles Cavendish's *Philosophical Letters*, writing that he trusts Conway will "smile" at the "conceit" of Cavendish's attempts to "confute" his work in her "large book." In a second letter, written in early May, he informs Conway that Cavendish has "sent two more folios of hers" to him, again "intended to confute" his views. "I believe she may be secure from anyone giving her the trouble of a reply," he sniffs.[209]

For his part, in the same year Mary Evelyn overheard him praising Margaret Cavendish, Walter Charleton wrote at some length to the duchess about her work, clearly having spent time with her books, and he carefully details his responses to her natural philosophy, her moral philosophy, and her poetry.[210] And in 1671, Thomas Shadwell turned the tables, sending Cavendish the gift of a play, *The Humorists*, which he hoped to dedicate to her, while apologizing that his request was, perhaps, "too great a presumption for me to hope that your grace (that makes so good use of your time with your own pen) can have so much to throw away as once to read this little offspring of mine." Her response was to send him a present, probably of her work: "to reward my crime [the

[208] Thomas Hobbes to Margaret Cavendish, 9 February 1661, in *Letters and Poems*, ed. William Cavendish, 67-68. I have silently modernized the spelling and punctuation.

[209] Henry More to Margaret Cavendish, [1664], in *Letters and Poems*, ed. William Cavendish, 90-91 For More's comments about Cavendish, see Henry More to Anne Conway, n. d. [April 1664], in *The Conway Letters: The Correspondence of Anne, Viscountess Conway, Henry More, and Their Friends, 1642-1684*, rev. ed. Marjorie Hope Nicholson and Sarah Hutton [New York: Oxford University Press, 1992], 234, 237. I have silently modernized the spelling and punctuation.

[210] Walter Charleton to Margaret Cavendish, 7 May 1667, in *Letters and Poems*, ed. William Cavendish, 108-19.

"presumption" of his dedication] is beyond expression generous," he replied.[211]

Cavendish also presented copies of her books to the colleges of Oxford and Cambridge, and today over one hundred presentation copies of her books are still in the Oxford libraries to which she donated them.[212] In surveying these presentation copies, William Poole observes, "Of the colleges and halls then extant, all received copies, and most still hold anywhere between two and nine of her early editions; and although not all these books came from Margaret herself, most did." And in Cambridge, Poole notes, "the picture is the same: the older college libraries are awash with Cavendish, perhaps even more so than their Oxonian cousins."[213] Her gifts produced many flattering and effusive letters of thanks in return—the flattery and effusion are not at all unusual in letters from beneficiaries to wealthy and noble patrons, which clearly the Cavendishes were—but very few of the letters that William Cavendish collected and published in his wife's honor after her death suggest the recipients had read Margaret's books.[214] It would be interesting to know what Cavendish herself made of the extravagant praises these letters contained. Some of the letters sent from the colleges, thanking her for her gifts, were accompanied by Latin versions in addition to the English, which must have been a source of some discomfort to Cavendish, aware, as she was, of her deficient education, in particular of the language of universal scholarship. Cavendish also disseminated her volumes beyond the English universities—a letter to her from Constantijn Huygens, dated 28 November 1658, informs Margaret that, "according to your excellency's command," he has presented her *Philosophical and Physical Opinions* to Leiden University.[215]

[211] Thomas Shadwell to Margaret Cavendish, 25 May 1671, in *Letters and Poems*, ed. William Cavendish, 130. I have silently modernized the spelling and punctuation.

[212] Poole, "Margaret Cavendish's Books," 2.

[213] Poole, "Margaret Cavendish's Books," 3.

[214] After his wife's death, William Cavendish included dozens of such letters from Oxford and Cambridge in *Letters and Poems*.

[215] Constantijn Huygens to Margaret Cavendish, 28 November 1658, in *Letters and Poems*, ed. William Cavendish, 102. I have silently modernized the spelling and punctuation. This is followed by a Latin letter of thanks addressed to "Illustrissima Domina," from the academic rector of the university. Margaret Cavendish's undated letter to Constantijn Huygens, accompanying her present of books, is in *Die Briefwisseling van Constantijn Huygens*, ed. Worp, 5:312.

(She responded by sending the university all of her books along with a specially prepared Latin index.[216])

The writer, philosopher, and clergyman Joseph Glanvill presented Cavendish with a copy of his book on witchcraft, and she thanked him by returning the favor, sending him what he described as her own "ingenious works." He did her the honor not only of writing to thank her for the present but also of replying in some detail to criticisms she offered of his work. He then asked her a favor "on public account": Bath had just "erected" a library, and as Glanvill notes, "there are in it several worthy authors, but it wants the great honor and ornament of the illustrious duchess of Newcastle's works." As a "humble solicitor," Glanvill hoped that she would favor the library at Bath just as she favored the many "considerable libraries of England," clearly those at Oxford and Cambridge.[217]

Cavendish also received letters of thanks for gifts of her "*oeuvres*" from the philosopher Samuel de Sorbière and from the Scottish physician William Davison, who signed himself "D. Avissone," both writing in French. Did these letters also serve as reminders of her linguistic deficiencies? Robert Creighton, a royalist exile living in Utrecht, also received a gift of books from Cavendish, or, rather, in his words, she "was pleased to appear" to him in "another dress, under the veil of books." Undoubtedly his praise is excessive: "Were those ancients now alive who first discoursed of atoms, matter, form, and other ingredients of the world's fabric, they would hang their heads, confounded to see a lady of most honorable extraction, in prime of youth, amidst a thousand fasheries [troubles, vexations] of greatness, say more of their own mysteries than they," he rhapsodizes. But he offered her one true nugget of thoughtfulness and comfort in response to her apologies for her own lack of any language other than English. "Those

---

[216] Constantijn Huygens to Margaret Cavendish, 2/12 August 1664, in *Die Briefwisseling van Constantijn Huygens*, ed. Worp, 6:88-89. I have silently modernized the spelling and punctuation.

[217] Joseph Glanvill to Margaret Cavendish, 22 December [1666?], n. d., and 25 August [1667?], in *Letters and Poems*, ed. William Cavendish, 85, 98-100, 103-4. Glanvill was rector of the Abbey Church in Bath from 1666 to 1680; his *Philosophical Considerations Touching the Being of Witches and Witchcraft* was published in 1666. Presumably his letters to Cavendish, one undated and two not fully dated, were written between 1666 and 1667. I have silently modernized the spelling and punctuation.

old philosophers too knew only their own tongue, Greek," he reminds her.[218]

While she was alive, Cavendish published no commendatory verses from colleagues in her folio collections of plays because she had no colleagues, aside from her husband, and no commendatory verses were written. One bit of verse, sent to her from Trinity College, Cambridge in 1668, might have served, a few lines intended as an "honorable monument" to her:

> To Margaret the First,
> Princess of Philosophers,
> Who hath dispelled errors,
> Appeased the differences of opinions,
> And restored peace
> To learning's commonwealth.[219]

She did not publish these lines, however flattering. But poems full of praise did come, at last, solicited or not, after her death, and they filled the last thirty pages of the book William Cavendish dedicated to his wife's memory. Poems in English and Latin, poems signed and unsigned, poems "to" her, poems about her, even one addressed to her "closet," described as a "sacred cell / Where holy hermits anciently did dwell." Poems comparing her to the Faerie Queene, to Dido, to Helen, poems that claim she broke the glass ceiling—or, rather, she "scaled the walls of fame, / And made a breach where never female came"—and poems that proclaim her as the tenth muse. Praises, elegies, epitaphs. And one, perhaps unconsciously reflecting Cavendish's singular gender-bending, observing that as long as she was alive, "wit was hermaphrodite," but "now 'tis only masculine again."[220] And yet, even in death, Cavendish was a target of ridicule. This mock epitaph was copied by John Stainsby, a law clerk, and sent on to his friend, the antiquarian Elias Ashmole:

---

[218] Robert Creighton to Margaret Cavendish, 1653, in *Letters and Poems*, ed. William Cavendish, 85-87. I have silently modernized the spelling and punctuation.

[219] Trinity College to Margaret Cavendish, 5 October 1668, in *Letters and Poems*, ed. William Cavendish, 152. I have silently modernized the spelling and punctuation.

[220] The poems are in *Poems and Letters*, ed. William Cavendish, 153-82. I have silently modernized the spelling and punctuation

"Here lies wise, chaste, hospitable, humble—"
I had gone on, but Nick [the devil] began to grumble:
"Write, write," says he, "upon her tomb of marble
These words, which out I and my friends will warble:
'Shame of her sex, Welbeck's illustrious whore,
The true man's hate and grief, plague of the poor,
The great atheistical philosophraster,
That owns no God, no devil, lord, nor master,
Vice's epitome and virtue's foe,
Here lies her body, but her soul's below."[221]

Still, there were a few readers who responded to Cavendish's work in print. The earliest of such responses came in 1657, notable not only because it was a public notice rather than a private note but because the critic was a woman, Suzanne Du Verger. Du Verger was a writer and translator who had published a collection of "histories" carefully edited from Jean-Pierre Camus's *Les Événements singuliers* and printed under the title *Admirable Events . . . together with Moral Relations* in 1639, a volume dedicated to Queen Henrietta Maria. In *Du Verger's Humble Reflections upon Some Passages of the Right Honorable the Lady Marchioness of Newcastle's Olio*, Du Verger addresses Cavendish directly.[222] As her title suggests, she takes issue with some of Cavendish's views, which she regards as "misinformed." In a dedicatory epistle, Du Verger praises Cavendish's "delicious and exquisite" *Olio*, elaborating on the literal meaning of the Spanish word for spicy stew and contrasting Cavendish's dainty dish, "delicately dressed, seasoned, and set out" with her "noble hand" to her own humbler and more "ordinary, poor fare." But after "greedily" eating the delicacies Cavendish has prepared, Du Verger says that she unexpectedly "met with morsels so willowish [ill-tasting] and un-sound," even "wholly corrupted," that she became nauseated and began to "loathe" what had formerly tasted so good. Du Verger's particular objection is to Cavendish's essay "On the Monastical Life."[223] In her

---

[221] Quoted in Grant, *Margaret the First*, 199, and in Whitaker, *Mad Madge*, 348. I have silently modernized the spelling and punctuation.

[222] *Du Vergers Humble Reflections upon some Passages of the right Honorable the Lady Marchionesse of Newcastles OLIO, or an Appeale from her Mes-informed, to her owne better informed judgement* (London, 1657).

[223] Cavendish, *The Worlds Olio*, 28-31.

Humble Reflections, Du Verger identifies points of contention, summarizes Cavendish's views, and then responds to each point, in turn, addressing a series of "paragraphs," reflections, and objections directly to Cavendish herself. The aim is to "correct" the inaccuracies and misrepresentations in Cavendish's essay with her own views of monasticism. Clearly Du Verger has not only *read* Cavendish, she takes her seriously, responding to the two-and-a-half folio pages of Cavendish's original essay with a hundred and sixty-eight octavo pages of her own.

And in 1673, the year of Cavendish's death, the early feminist Bathsua Makin published *An Essay to Revive the Ancient Education of Gentlewomen*, in which she praises Cavendish as a woman who, "by her own genius, rather than any timely instruction, overtops many grave gown-men." Makin lists Cavendish, along with such female notables as the humanist scholar Olympia Morata, Elizabeth Tudor, Jane Grey, and Christina of Sweden, among others, as women who were "educated in arts and tongues" and recognized as "eminent in them."[224] Two years later, there was another note of recognition when the critic and author Edward Phillips included Margaret Cavendish in his *Theatrum Poetarum Anglicanorum*, a comprehensive survey of English poets, describing her as "a very obliging lady to the world" who had "largely and copiously impart[ed] to public view her studious endeavors in the arts and ingenuities."[225] Interestingly, however, Phillips notes only "three ample volumes in print": "one of orations, the other of philosophical notions and discourses, the third of dramatic and other kinds of poetry." From these very general descriptions of Cavendish's "ample volumes," it's hard to tell which of her books he may have had in mind, or whether he was actually familiar with any of them.

As the seventeenth century drew to a close, the biographer and critic of stage drama Gerard Langbaine included Margaret Cavendish (as well

---

[224] *An Essay to Revive the Antient Education of Gentlewomen in Religion, Manners, Arts, & Tongues . . .* (London, 1673), in *First Feminist: British Women Writers, 1578-1799*, ed. Moira Ferguson (Bloomington: Indiana University Press, 1985), 132. I have silently modernized the spelling and punctuation.

[225] Edward Phillips, *Theatrum poetarum anglicanorum, or a Compleat Collection of the Poets . . .* (London, 1675), 2:48. The book contains two "volumes," and only the second "volume" is paginated. Here, Cavendish and other female writers are separated from male poets and placed in a list headed "Women." I have silently modernized the spelling and punctuation.

as her husband) in his *Account of the English Dramatic Poets*.[226] Langbaine had more than a passing familiarity with Cavendish's work. He writes that, "her soul sympathizing" with her husband's "in all things, especially in dramatic poetry," she published "twenty-six plays besides several loose scenes" in two collections. However, Langbaine declines to pass judgment on her writing even as he points out that "some have but a mean opinion of her plays." In Cavendish's defense Langbaine notes, "if it be considered that both the language and the plots of them are all her own, I think she ought with justice be preferred to others of her sex, which have built their fame on other people's foundations." To illustrate her originality, he quotes from the "General Prologue" to her 1662 *Plays*, where Cavendish contrasted her plays to those of Jonson, Shakespeare, and Beaumont and Fletcher, who relied on sources for their plots. Langbaine's entry on Cavendish includes an alphabetized list of her plays, describing each title's genre and frequently adding some additional descriptive information, such as "this play consists of three and twenty scenes but is not divided into acts" (about *Apocryphal Ladies*) and "His Grace writ the epilogue to the first part" (about the two-part comedy *The Play Called Wit's Cabal*). The entry for *The Female Academy* is very brief, noting only Langbaine's decision about the play's genre: "a comedy." His "account" of Cavendish ends with a brief bibliography of her non-dramatic work.

In the eighteenth century, the legal writer and would-be poet Giles Jacob (who, unfortunately for him, figured as one of the dunces in Alexander Pope's *Dunciad*) included an entry on Margaret Cavendish in his two-volume *Poetical Register*, describing her as "the most voluminous dramatic writer of our female poets."[227] Although Jacob judges Cavendish to have "a more than ordinary propensity to dramatic poetry," for the rest of his entry he simply reproduces Langbaine's list of plays, noting his source

---

[226] Gerard Langbaine, *An Account of the English Dramatick Poets, or, Some Observations and Remarks on the Lives and Writings of all those that have Published either Comedies, Tragi-Comedies, Pastorals, Masques, Interludes, Farces, or Opera's in the English Tongue* (Oxford, 1691), 390-94. I have included the full title to show the comprehensive nature of Langbaine's effort. In quoting from his work, I have silently modernized the spelling and punctuation.

[227] Giles Jacob, *The Poetical Register: or, the Lives and Characters of All the English Poets, with an Account of their Writings* (London, 1723), 2:190-92. I have silently modernized the spelling and punctuation.

and adding "all the language and plots of her plays, Mr. Langbaine tells us, were her own." He rearranges Langbaine's list, however—in Jacob's list, the plays are neither alphabetically nor chronologically arranged, and he reduces the number to nineteen rather than Langbaine's twenty-six. Like Langbaine, Jacob follows his discussion of the plays with brief comments about additional work published by Cavendish, but where Langbaine included eight titles in total, Jacob reduces the number to three: a book of poems (the title of which he did not give), her biography of her husband, and her own autobiography. Aside from his claims that Cavendish was the "most voluminous" female dramatist and that she had a natural inclination to the writing of drama, there was nothing new in Jacob's discussion of Cavendish and no indication that he was personally familiar with any of her plays.

When the historian George Ballard came to write a profile of Cavendish some thirty years later, in his 1752 *Memoirs of Several Ladies of Great Britain Who Have Been Celebrated for Their Writings or Skill in the Learned Language and Sciences*, he relied for much of his information on Langbaine and Jacob.[228] Ballard's focus was principally on biography, not criticism, and in writing about Margaret Cavendish, he tamed the story of her life. In Ballard's retelling, the young Margaret Lucas's rather limited education becomes a "remarkably careful . . . education." He also asserts that the young woman was taught "the French tongue," which, as we have seen, Cavendish did not know. (Though Ballard did lament that Cavendish did not have training in the "learned languages," Greek and Latin.) Interestingly, however, while Ballard relied on Langbaine and Jacob for a critical assessment of Cavendish's work, he seems to have searched out her volumes himself, since he describes drawing up a "catalogue of all her works which have come to my knowledge"; living in Oxford, he may well have been able to locate many of the volumes Cavendish had donated to the various colleges. The list he annotates is fascinating: about *The World's Olio*, he writes, "which I have not seen yet"; about *Observations upon Experimental Philosophy*," he notes, "Mr. James Bristow began to translate some of those philosophical discourses into the Latin tongue."[229] Ballard includes her 1662 *Plays* in his Cavendish

[228] George Ballard, *Memoirs of Several Ladies of Great Britain* (Oxford, 1752), 299-306. In quoting from Ballard, I have silently modernized the spelling and punctuation.

[229] James Bristow, a scholar from Christ Church, had been "commissioned to Latinize Margaret's philosophy," but "abandoned the project 'finding great difficulties

bibliography, but about the 1668 *Plays, Never before Printed*, he writes, "this book I have not seen." He relied on Langbaine for his information about Cavendish's dramatic works, however, simply listing her plays "in the same order that gentleman placed them." Indeed, by the time Ballard was searching out information about Cavendish, it wasn't even clear when she had died—the date wasn't on her monument in Westminster Abbey, and Ballard could only find it by consulting one "Mr. Fuhrman, in the fifteenth volume of his manuscript collections in Corpus Christi College archives."

A year later, the actor and playwright Theophilus Cibber (son of the much more famous playwright and poet-laureate Colley Cibber) published *Lives of the Poets of Great Britain and Ireland, to the Time of Dean Swift*. Cibber cites Langbaine and Jacob for much of his information about Cavendish, but he also expands biographical details he must have found in Ballard, adding that Cavendish's mother "was remarkably assiduous" in her children's education, for example, and that "her trouble in cultivating this daughter's mind was not in vain, for she discovered early an inclination to learning." Cibber also adds to the story of the Cavendish-Lucas courtship an anecdote about Margaret's brother. In Cibber's telling, Charles Lucas had told William "he was not solicitous about his own affairs, for he knew the worst could be but suffering either death or exile in the royal cause, but his chief solicitude was for his sister, on whom he could bestow no fortune and whose beauty exposed her to danger." This "raised the marquis's curiosity to see her and from that circumstance arose the marquis's affection to this lady." Cibber has little to say about Cavendish's writing, simply noting that, after the Restoration, "she dedicated her time to writing poems, philosophical discourses, orations, and plays," and adding that "though she was very beautiful, she died without issue." He quotes Jacob on her productivity and "propensity," and Langbaine on the originality of her plots, and although he quotes, almost verbatim, Ballard's search for the date of her death (down to the reference to Fuhrman and his "fifteenth volume") and reproduces almost exactly Ballard's bibliography of Cavendish's works, he does not name Ballard as a source.[230]

---

therein, through the confusedness of the matter.'" Quoted in Whitaker, *Mad Madge*, 256.

[230] Theophilus Cibber, *The Lives of the Poets of Great Britain and Ireland* (London, 1753), 2:162-69. Cibber clearly relied on Ballard elsewhere; in the biography of Katherine

With the exception of her biography of her husband, none of Cavendish's books had been—or would be—republished after her death, but a small selection of her poetry was included in the 1755 anthology *Poems by Eminent Ladies* edited by George Colman, an essayist and dramatist, and Bonnell Thornton, a poet and essayist.[231] The two repeat the mistake, first made by Ballard, that Margaret was the youngest child of *Charles* Lucas; according to their brief biographical note, "it is plain, from the uncommon turn of her compositions, that she possessed a wild native genius." They lament the fact that this "native genius" clearly had not been "duly cultivated," thus preventing Cavendish's poetry from "show[ing] itself to advantage in the higher sorts of poetry." *Poems by Eminent Ladies* contains "Melancholy and Mirth" and "Peace and War," both dialogues; a poem about death, headed "Nature's Cook"; and a poem titled "Wit." The two longest selections in the anthology focus on fairies: "The Pastime and Recreation of the Queen of the Fairies in Fairyland, the Center of the Earth" and "The Pastime of the Queen of the Fairies, When She First Comes upon Earth out of the Center." All of these are from Cavendish's 1653 *Poems and Fancies*, although, as Katie Whitaker notes, Colman and Thornton carefully trimmed Cavendish's poems by "omitting those sections that offended against the editors' sense of decency," and omitting, too, any "comment whatsoever to tell the readers what they had done." In the "Pastime and Recreation," for example, "the two editors cut out the grotesquerie of Margaret's description of the fairies' diet—including ants' eggs, flies, and dormouse milk—and of the mischief they practiced on humans."[232] And while Colman produced plays and managed the Covent Garden Theatre, there is no reference in this anthology to any of Cavendish's plays.

Cavendish made a brief appearance in Horace Walpole's *Catalogue of the Royal and Noble Authors of England, Scotland, and Ireland*, first published in 1758.[233] A well-known playwright, historian, and novelist, the author mostly famously of the gothic *Castle of Otranto*, Walpole includes an entry

---

Philips, for example, which immediately precedes Cavendish's, Cibber adds a footnote citing "Ballard's *Memoirs*"). I have silently modernized the spelling and punctuation.

[231] George Colman and Bonnell Thornton, eds., *Poems by Eminent Ladies* (London, 1755), 2:197-212. I have silently modernized the spelling and punctuation.

[232] Whitaker, *Mad Madge*, 352.

[233] Horace Walpole, *Catalogue of the Royal and Noble Authors of England, Scotland, and Ireland*, ed. Thomas Park (London, 1806), 145-56.

for Margaret Cavendish among his "royal and noble authors," first listing her works and then concluding this bibliography with a bit of an insult: "Whoever has a mind to know more of this fertile pedant will find a detail of her works in Ballard's *Memoirs*, from whence I have taken this account." Walpole follows this with a few biographical and critical comments, including a long extract from "The Pastime and Recreation of the Queen of Fairies in Fairyland, the Center of the Earth" (from *Poems and Fancies*) as an example of "her grace's happier efforts," and then a passage from "Epistle to My Brain" (from *Philosophical Fancies*), which, he says, "may be cited as an aggregate of much metrical obscurity." A few pages later, Walpole sets out to write about William Cavendish, but he can't quite draw himself away from the duke's wife and offers a few remarks about the "fantastic couple," the duke and his "faithful duchess"—Walpole regards many of Margaret's judgments in her biography of her husband to be "amusing," and he is quick to observe that, "though she had written philosophy, it seems she had read none." She had an "unbounded passion for scribbling." (To be fair, he also regarded William Cavendish as "a man in whose character ridicule would find more materials than satire.") About the couple, Walpole concludes, "What a picture of foolish nobility was this stately poetic couple, retired to their own little domain, and intoxicating one another with circumstantial flattery, on what was of consequence to no mortal but themselves!"[234] Aside from his jibes, Walpole offers little new information in his account of Cavendish, drawing liberally not only on Ballard but also on Langbaine, Jacob, and Cibber, all of whom he cites.

Cavendish's name continued to appear regularly in biographical encyclopedias. Although she was not included in Alexander Chalmers's bestselling *New and General Biographical Dictionary* (her husband was), she did appear in *Biographium Faemineum: The Female Worthies*, a collection of "memoirs of the most illustrious ladies of all ages and nations" published in 1766.[235] While the encyclopedia contained an entry for "Newcastle, Margaret (duchess of)," all of the information is recycled, almost verbatim, from Langbaine and Jacob. But along the way, all criticism of Cavendish has been excised, leaving her as a perfect paragon: "In her person she was noble and graceful; in her temper, shy and reserved; in

---

[234] Walpole, *Catalogue*, 189-205

[235] *Biographium Faemineum: The Female Worthies, or, Memoirs of the Most Illustrious Ladies, of All Ages and Nations* . . . (London, 1766).

her studies, contemplations, and writings, indefatigable." She was, in sum, "pious, generous, and charitable," an "excellent economist," "kind to her servants," and a "perfect pattern of conjugal love and duty."[236]

There is also a brief entry for "Margaret, dutchess of Newcastle" in James Granger's *A Biographical History of England, from Egbert the Great to the Revolution*, first published in 1769. Included in his alphabetical list of "poetesses," the clergyman and critic observes about Cavendish, "If her merit as an author were to be estimated from the *quantity* of her works, she would have the precedence of all female writers, ancient or modern." But, while he regards Cavendish's biography of her husband to be "estimable," the rest of her work is not, at least in his view. While noting that there are "no less than thirteen folios of her writing," Granger concludes, "We are greatly surprised that a lady of her quality should have written so much; and are little less surprised that one who loved writing so well, has writ no better." And what "is most to be wondered at" is that "she, who found so much time for writing, could acquit herself in the several duties and regulations of life, with so much propriety."[237]

As the nineteenth century began, Margaret Cavendish did not rate an entry in the wonderfully title *Eccentric Biography, or Memoirs of Remarkable Female Characters Ancient and Modern, Including Actresses, Adventurers, Authoresses, Fortunetellers, Gypsies, Dwarfs, Swindlers and Vagrants* published in 1803. Given the pervasive skeptical views of Cavendish, it's probably just as well. But she did find a place in one of the rare biographical encyclopedias compiled by a woman, *Memoirs of Celebrated Female Characters*, published in 1804 by the poet and novelist Mary Pilkington.[238] The entry reproduces earlier errors, for example the claim that Cavendish was the daughter of Charles Lucas, and Pilkington adds this about Cavendish's mother: "Few women were more capable of the task of education than lady Lucas, and her daughters were allowed to be the most accomplished females of the age." Nothing in Cavendish's autobiography suggests anything of the sort about Elizabeth Lucas's

---

[236] *Biographium Faemineum*, 149-51

[237] James Granger, *A Biographical History of England, from Egbert the Great to the Revolution* (London, 1769), 4:60-61.

[238] Mrs. [Mary] Pilkington, *Memoirs of Celebrated Female Characters, Who Have Distinguished Themselves by Their Talents and Virtues in Every Age and Nation* (London: Albion Press, 1804), 272-73.

capacities for (or interest in) educating her daughters. But Pilkington was more than charitable to Cavendish and her work, perhaps sympathetic to the hostility a woman like the duchess experienced. "Though their biographers have ridiculed the scribbling mania which seized them," she writes about William and Margaret Cavendish, "it afforded them a degree of happiness which very few attain." Pilkington does not add a detailed bibliography of works by Margaret Cavendish, however, noting that to "specify the various performances of this fertile author, would give a work so concise as this, the appearance of a bookseller's catalogue of sale," adding, in a sad note, "as they scarcely outlived the memory of their illustrious composer, the account would not be likely to entertain." Of the wealth of Cavendish's literary production, Pilkington includes only seventeen lines from "Dialogue between Melancholy and Mirth," a poem from *Nature's Pictures* that extends over some five pages in the original.

Just a few years later, the first edited collection of Margaret Cavendish's poetry appeared. In 1813, Egerton Brydges published *Select Poems of Margaret Cavendish, Duchess of Newcastle*, a slim volume only twenty pages long.[239] Like Colman and Thornton, Brydges ignores Cavendish's philosophy and science writing, her essays, her epistles, and her plays, restricting himself to publishing a selection of her poetry. In the "advertisement" prefacing the poems, Brydges defends Cavendish, "whose genius has been decried and ridiculed," even while admitting that there are "many absurd passages in many of Her grace's compositions." But, while defending Cavendish's genius and granting that she had an "active, thinking, and original mind" as well as an imagination that was "quick, copious, and sometimes even beautiful," he condemns her "taste." It was "not only uncultivated, but perhaps originally defective." "Nothing that I have read of hers, [sic] is touched by pathos," he sniffs, adding, "we are too frequently shocked by expressions and images of extraordinary coarseness; and more extraordinary as flowing from a female of high rank, brought up in courts." He can't publish her poetry without offering, in his notes, his own suggestions about the ways it could be improved. About a line in "A Dialogue between Melancholy and Mirth," for instance, he writes, "This and the nineteen following

---

[239] Egerton Brydges, ed., *Select Poems of Margaret Cavendish, Duchess of Newcastle* (Kent, UK: Lee Priory Press, 1813). At the end of his prefatory "Advertisement" (n.p.), Brydges notes "From her the Editor of these Poems is proud to record his descent."

lines are highly spirited and beautiful, and prove the Duchess to have felt at times the inspiration of real genius, which only wanted the pruning hand of a more correct judgment." And a few lines later: "In these days it seems a little wonderful that a lady of rank so high, and mind so cultivated, could use language so coarse and disgusting as is seen here." Still, and uniquely, this volume contained two brief lyrics from *The Convent of Pleasure*, titled by Brydges "Song of the Princess, in the Character of a Shepherd: Answered by Lady Happy" and "Song of the Lady Happy."[240]

One intriguing reference to Cavendish—elusive in its vagueness and unusual in its personal appreciation—is found in Charles Lamb's *Essays of Elia*, published in 1823, though the essays themselves first began appearing in *The London Magazine* in 1820. In these essays, Lamb presented himself as Elia, his sister Mary as Cousin Bridget. In "Mackery End, in Hertfordshire," Lamb/Elia writes that he and his "housekeeper," Bridget, live "generally in harmony" with only "occasional bickerings—as it should be among near relatives." One of their points of difference lies in their literary tastes: "I can pardon her blindness to the beautiful obliquities of the *Religion Medici*, but she must apologize to me for certain disrespectful insinuations which she has been pleased to throw out latterly touching the intellectuals of a dear favorite of mine of the last century but one, the thrice noble, chaste, and virtuous, but again somewhat fantastical and original-brained, generous Margaret Newcastle."[241]

There are several other references to Cavendish in Lamb's essays. Earlier, in "The Two Races of Men," Lamb embarked on a bit of a rant about "those who borrow" and "those who lend," directing his anger especially at those who borrowed books and failed to return them. In the essay, he imagines addressing one of those borrowers who offended him: "But what moved thee, wayward, spiteful K., to be so importunate to carry off with thee, in spite of tears and adjurations to thee to forbear, the *Letters* of that princely woman, the thrice-noble Margaret Newcastle,

---

[240] The two lyrics from *The Convent of Pleasure* are in Brydges, *Select Poems*, 10-12 and 16-17. In the play itself, these lyrics appear in 4.1 and 1.2.; see Cavendish, *The Convent of Pleasure*, ed. Sharon L. Jansen (Saltar's Point Press, 2016).

[241] Charles Lamb, *Essays of Elia* (1823; New York: D. Appleton, 1879), 121-22. I have silently modernized the punctuation. *Religio Medici* (*The Religion of a Doctor*) is Sir Thomas Browne's long religious testament, first published in 1643.

knowing at the time, and knowing that I knew also, thou most assuredly wouldst never turn over one leaf of the illustrious folio?" Even worse, K. had taken the book to France![242] In "The Complaint of the Decay of Beggars in the Metropolis," Cavendish is just an aside, where Elia refers to the "poets and romancical writers," adding "(as dear Margaret Newcastle would call them)."[243] When Lamb published a second series of essays ten years later, the *Last Essays of Elia*, Cavendish was still with him. In "Detached Thoughts on Books and Reading," Lamb makes it a point to scoff at bad books that have been beautifully bound, and when he turns to Cavendish, you might cringe, thinking that he is about to poke fun at the duchess's lavish folio volumes. Instead, he uses Cavendish's biography of her husband as an example of a book that is both "good and rare." For such a volume, he says, "no casket is rich enough, no casing sufficiently durable, to honour and keep safe such a jewel."[244] His fascination with and appreciation for Cavendish seem genuine and enduring. Lamb is also said to have entertained his guests one evening by posing a topic for discussion: "persons one would wish to have seen." While his companions suggest John Locke and Isaac Newton, Shakespeare, Chaucer, Petrarch, and Dante, Henry Fielding and Samuel Richardson, among many other famous men, "Lamb impatiently declared for the duchess of Newcastle."[245]

Margaret Cavendish is also noted in Robert Watt's four-volume *Bibliotheca Britannica*, published in 1824.[246] There is little detail about her, except for her place of birth, the year of her death, and the description "a useful literary character." As with all of the other 40,000 entries in this massive series, what follows that brief note is a list of the titles of her works and their dates of publication. In addition to Cavendish's inclusion in biographical and bibliographical catalogues like Watt's, at least a bit of her poetry continued to appear in edited collections

---

[242] Lamb, *Essays of Elia*, 45. I have silently modernized the punctuation.

[243] Lamb, *Essays of Elia*, 184. I have silently modernized the punctuation.

[244] Lamb, *The Essays of Elia*, ed. Alfred Ainger (New York: A. C. Armstrong & Son, 1888), 220. I have silently modernized the punctuation.

[245] This account of an evening's conversation in 1814 is by William Hazlitt, quoted in Edward V. Lucas, *The Life of Charles Lamb*, 4th ed. (London: Methuen, 1907), 287. (The entire conversation is summarized on pp. 280-87).

[246] Robert Watt, *Bibliotheca Britannica, or, a General Index on the Literature of Great Britain and Ireland Ancient and Modern including Such Foreign Books as have been translated into English or printed in the British Dominions* . . . (Edinburgh: Archibald Constable, 1824), 1:204-5.

throughout the century. In his 1825 *Specimens of British Poetesses*, Alexander Dyce published not just an extract from but the complete "Pastime and Recreation of the Queen of the Fairies," adding in a note that previously published versions were "considerably curtailed" from the original.[247] But, while he includes the entire poem, he feels the need to add, "it would be difficult to point out a composition, which contains a more extraordinary mixture of imagination and coarse absurdity." Aside from six lines on "the theme of love" and eight lines of "The Funeral of Calamity" (from *Poems and Fancies*) the only other Cavendish poem in Dyce's anthology is one we have seen repeatedly, an extract from the "Dialogue of Melancholy and Mirth."

In 1848, the American preacher George Washington Bethune published three brief selections from Cavendish's work in *The British Female Poets with Biographical and Critical Notes*, extracts from "The Pastime and Recreation of the Queen of Fairies" and the dialogue "Melancholy and Mirth," just sixty-two lines in total from all the poetry Cavendish had published over the course of her writing career. In the biographical note, in which he cites Brydges as his source, Bethune observes, "Certainly nothing can exceed her or his [William Cavendish's] vanity, except the flattery they bestowed upon one another."[248] A year later, Frederick Rowton includes a few lyrics by Cavendish in his landmark anthology, *Female Poets of Great Britain*. In a brief headnote, he observes that Cavendish's husband "assisted her in her literary labours" and judges that, while she was ambitious, none of her "plays, poems, orations, and essays" is remarkable "for wit or genius."[249]

Meanwhile, for Louisa Stuart Costello, who published the multi-volume *Memoirs of Eminent Englishwomen*, Margaret Cavendish is the perfect example of a woman who had "some talent and no genius," one of those women who "contrive to bring themselves into notice by dint of resolute scribbling, and manage to attain a certain reputation by means of frequent assurances to the world that they deserve a high place in

---

[247] Alexander Dyce, *Specimens of British Poetesses*, 2nd ed. (London: T. Rodd, 1827), 88-98.

[248] George W. Bethune, *The British Female Poets with Biographical and Critical Notes* (1848; Philadelphia: Lindsay and Blakiston, 1856), 35-38.

[249] Frederick Rowton, *The Female Poets of Great Britain* (Philadelphia: Carey and Hart, 1849), 79-82.

public estimation."[250] Costello dismisses Cavendish as a nuisance, as vain, as ignorant (suggesting that Cavendish was too dim to realize she was being ridiculed), and as a woman foolishly "pluming" herself on her husband's literary reputation—but, since Costello includes many disparaging comments about William Cavendish as a writer, it's hard to see exactly how Margaret could have been "pluming" herself on his reputation. In compiling her bibliography of Margaret's work, Costello cites Walpole and Brydges, quoting their comments about Cavendish at some length, but she does seem to add her own views about selections from *The World's Olio*, *The Blazing World*, and Cavendish's auto-biographical *True Relation*, so it may well be that she had actually read some Cavendish rather than contenting herself with recapitulating previous treatments of the work. However, Costello reproduces only a brief passage from Cavendish's poem on wit, a selection from "The Pastime and Recreation of the Queen of the Fairies," and a part of the "Dialogue between Melancholy and Mirth."

The first really significant publication of Cavendish material is Edward Jenkins's *A Cavalier and His Lady: Selections from the First Duke and Duchess of Newcastle*.[251] In his introductory essay, Jenkins stresses his unique efforts: "I warrant," he writes, "few have ever seen one of her folios, and hardly any one ever reads them. Many of them are rarer than gold. . . . Perhaps I have read them more and oftener than any other curious bookworm of these days, and amongst sad heaps of rubbish it has seemed to me there are a few treasures well worth disinterment." Jenkins seems to have owned at least one of Cavendish's books—he recalls that, after reading Lamb's praise of Cavendish's life of her husband, "I had that first-mentioned jewel lying in a dirty buff casket on my shelf." He also sought out and read *Poems and Fancies*, *The World's Olio*, *Philosophical and Physical Opinions*, *Nature's Pictures*, and the *CCXI Sociable Letters*. He calls his efforts "discouraging," noting in particular all the prefaces ("numerous, apologetic, remonstrative, defensive, discursive, grotesque"), regards some of her "philosophical opinions" as "madder than those of an Alexandrian gnostic or a medieval dreamer," and sums it all up as a great "chaos" of work. "Nevertheless," he concludes,

---

[250] Louisa Stuart Costello, *Memoirs of Eminent Englishwomen* (London: Richard Bentley, 1844), 3:211-35.

[251] Edward Jenkins, ed., *A Cavalier and His Lady: Selections from the First Duke and Duchess of Newcastle* (London: Macmillan, 1872).

"wherever one reads in the Duchess's books, he finds the tokens of a lively, vigorous, exuberant fancy and an ingenious wit," "here and there good strokes of dry sarcastic humour," "often thoughts of great force and beauty," and "many felicitous thoughts and expressions."

But Jenkins can't end his preface on an entirely positive note: "In every page there are things offensive to a fastidious or even an ordinarily healthy taste." Her images too frequently display "extreme coarseness." And Jenkins condemns the "absurd and audacious" poems addressed to her after her death, collected, and published by William Cavendish. Though she had been dubbed "the mad duchess," Jenkins concludes that Cavendish was "harmless," perhaps the most dismissive charge of all. But rather than simply reprinting the same two poems we have seen so many times before, he publishes her autobiography in its entirety, sixty pages of her poetry, Lady Happy's speech about men from the second scene of *The Convent of Pleasure*, sixty pages of "allegories, essays and aphorisms," and twenty-two of her "sociable letters." Indeed, despite the subtitle of the volume, the anthology is far more Margaret Cavendish's than it is her husband's—fewer than forty pages of the "selections" come from William Cavendish's poetry, nothing at all from his masterwork on horsemanship.

About nineteenth-century attitudes toward Cavendish, Katie Whitaker writes that, as "critics crew increasingly aware of Margaret's deviations from contemporary taste, she came to be seen as a woman of bizarre character." She became "an inspired, but utterly fantastic figure."[252] Such a view of Cavendish—he even uses the word *bizarrerie* to describe her "mode of working"—is reflected in Eric Robertson's *English Poetesses: A Series of Critical Biographies*, published as the nineteenth century drew to an end.[253] Robertson begins his discussion of Cavendish by comparing her to Aphra Behn—in contrast to Behn, he writes, Cavendish has been "treated" to the "sneer of the dissolute" at her "pretensions to innocence," which Robertson seems to suggest is unfair.

---

[252] Whitaker, *Mad Madge*, 353-54. Whitaker has also tracked down—or attempted to track down—the source of the unfortunate nickname "Mad Madge of Newcastle," first recorded by Mark Anthony Lower in his 1872 preface to a new edition of Margaret's biography of her husband. Whitaker searched in vain for any source for the nickname, concluding that "there might well be no seventeenth-century source for the Mad Madge nickname" (p. 355).

[253] Eric Robertson, *English Poetesses: A Series of Critical Biographies* (London: Cassell, 1883), 13-34.

Nevertheless, he regards the "frankness of her disclosures with respect to herself" as "embarrassing," though he grudgingly admits that her "artless candour" and her conceit combine to disarm criticisms. In detailing the many failings of her writing, he notes that one of the sentences in her *True Relation* "is twelve pages long" (something I certainly failed to note as a reader), and that the contents of her books are so jumbled they look like nothing so much as "a lady's overturned work-basket."

One of Robertson's most interesting judgments about Cavendish is that she was "a kind of over-grown, spoilt girl"; such infantilization seems to be intended as a way of smoothing over the oddities of her behavior, for Robertson is not entirely critical of Cavendish. He has consulted Jenkins's edition of Cavendish's work, and he is clearly familiar with Lamb's Elia essays, noting that "no later critic has supported in writing the emphatic praises of Elia." And so, Robertson is forced to "confess, with the object of surprising many readers with a style not far removed from Lamb himself," that he "cannot refrain from at once quoting a specimen of the Duchess's prose." What follows is an essay from *The World's Olio*, previously published by Jenkins, Cavendish's "Of Gentlewomen That are Sent to Board Schools."[254]

In addition to this essay, he includes selections from her *True Relation* and from her biography of her husband, both woven into his biographical narrative. He recognizes that, of all her verse, only "The Pastime of the Queen of the Fairies" and the "Dialogue between Melancholy and Mirth" were at all well known, but he nevertheless reprints portions of both, as well as Lady Happy's song from the *Convent of Pleasure*, though it is clear from his brief remarks about the play that he has not read it. Robertson also claims that, at times, Cavendish achieves "smooth passages" in her work, passages in which her "diction is almost as perfect as that which the most fastidious artifice could have devised," reproducing in his work a few of the "aphorisms" that Jenkins had printed in *The Cavalier and His Lady*. For Robertson, Cavendish's "aphoristic tendency" is "quite masculine; in his judgement it is "Baconian, almost."

---

[254] Cavendish, *The Worlds Olio*, 61-62. On this essay, see above, 66-67.

Unlike so many women writers before her, Margaret Cavendish and her work never completely disappeared from view, but her reputation was certainly tattered before the twentieth century began, and the first two books about her in the new century did not do anything to change the earlier critical views. In his 1910 *The First Duke and Duchess of Newcastle-upon-Tyne*, Thomas Longueville published a book-length study of the pair, drawing a great deal of his information about the duke from Margaret's biography of her husband.[255] In addition to his biographical narrative, Longueville devotes two chapters to William's writing, followed by two chapters that focus on Margaret's. He relies primarily on Langbaine, adding in comments by Cibber and Lamb. Longueville's judgments are not enthusiastic; he expresses a degree of appreciation for Cavendish's *Life*, noting it as a rich source of information about William Cavendish, but about the best he can muster about the rest of the duchess's work is a less-than-halfhearted and back-handed compliment: "It would be easy to sneer at her poetry," he says, "but, at its best, it is not so very bad."[256] He includes some lines from "The Pastime of the Queen of the Fairies" and some from "Melancholy and Mirth," which by 1910 had been published and republished many times, before slamming the poems praising the duchess published by William Cavendish after his wife's death. But here he resorts to quoting the eighteenth-century clergyman James Grainger, who had judged the volume to be filled with "the grossest and most fulsome panegyric" and who had concluded, "I know no flattery, ancient or modern, that is, in any degree, comparable to it, except the deification of Augustus and the erection of altars to him in his lifetime."[257]

Uniquely, however, at least up to this point in discussions of Cavendish's work, Longueville devotes an entire chapter to Cavendish's plays—or, rather, what he regards as the "formidable array" of her plays. He begins by citing a dozen lines from her "General Prologue" in the 1662 *Plays*, judging them to be "not the happiest of her poetical efforts," though he also acknowledges that since "even Dryden" failed in writing a prologue, perhaps "we may well make excuses" for Cavendish. The

---

[255] Thomas Longueville, *The First Duke and Duchess of Newcastle-upon-Tyne* (London: Longmans, Green, 1910).

[256] Longueville, *The First Duke and Duchess*, 254.

[257] Quoted in Longueville, *The First Duke and Duchess*, 258. For the original, see Granger, *Biographical History*, 4:61n.

lines he reproduces are those where Cavendish compared herself to Jonson, Shakespeare, and Beaumont and Fletcher; because she did not know Greek and Latin and thus did not have access to their sources, she argues that she couldn't "steal" the "wit" or the plots of those sources, as her male predecessors had.[258] To Cavendish's assertions, Longueville responds, in an aghast note, "Is this a slap on Shakespeare?" Immediately following, he prints three selected scenes from her plays: to illustrate her "heavy, wearisome style," he includes a scene from *The Presence*; to illustrate her "attempts at comedy," one from *The Bridals*; and to show her wit, one from *The Wit's Cabal*.

But, while Longueville at least *considers* Cavendish's dramatic efforts, his conclusions about her plays are entirely negative. Even "the most lenient official censor of our generation would certainly refuse to allow them to be acted," he opines, adding that they "combine indecency and obscenity with the stagnate dullness so usually the accompaniment of literary ditchwater." He follows up this very brief look at only a three of her plays (he began his bibliography by quoting Langbaine's list of all the titles of her plays, so he knew the extent of her dramatic output) with a series of anecdotes and comments drawn from her correspondents and contemporaries, giving particular emphasis to Pepys's gossipy diary entries, and finishing off with a terrible anecdote about Cavendish that, he admits, is not really about Cavendish at all but about someone else entirely. Even knowing that, this mistold story is Longueville's final word on the duchess of Newcastle—and he notes the misidentification only in a footnote.[259]

In another dual study of Margaret Cavendish and her husband, Henry Ten Eyck Perry gives Margaret preeminence: *The First Duchess of Newcastle and Her Husband as Figures in Literary History*. As Perry tells us in his introduction, the book began as his Harvard Ph.D. dissertation and was published as a monograph "in substantially its original form."[260]

---

[258] See above, 60-61.

[259] For the chapter on Cavendish's plays, Longueville, *The First Duke and Duchess*, 262-72. The anecdote Longueville recounts (271-72) involved a story about an event at court and a fantastically attired woman, a "devil of a phantom in masquerade." A "smart and amusing courtier" described the woman's outrageous costume to the king, who supposedly replied, "I bet . . . that it is the Duchess of Newcastle." It wasn't—"It turned out to be somebody else," Longueville writes.

[260] Henry Ten Eyck Perry, *The First Duchess of Newcastle and Her Husband as Figures in Literary History* (Boston: Ginn, 1918).

Interestingly, Perry conducted much of his research "on this side of the Atlantic," that is, in North America; he often found, to his surprise, that he could locate only one copy of some of Cavendish's works, and that lone copy was discovered with "exceeding difficulty." Fortunately he was given access to several of Cavendish's books in Henry E. Huntington's personal library, then in New York—thus documenting something of the dissemination of Cavendish's published volumes.[261] Perry's introduction is generous in its assessment of Cavendish; while she can be "verbose and tiresome," she is also "at times stimulating and readable." Like so many of his predecessors, Perry regards her best work as her biography of William Cavendish, though he judges it to be less a history and more "an early species of glory-story," arguing that it was written in a period "when fictitious material was beginning to masquerade as veracious record." As the *Life* was both literature and history, Perry thus devotes the first chapter of his book to an extended analysis of the life of William Cavendish as portrayed in *The Life of William Cavendish*.

After spending the following chapter on the work of William Cavendish, Perry then moves on to Margaret Cavendish's, an analysis of which occupies the rest of his literary study. In his view, the real significance of her literary productions lay in their quantity, not their quality—the value "does not consist in form or contents, but in the mere fact that they exist." Perry fully recognizes the almost insurmountable obstacles for early-modern women writers: "one needs to remember that masterpieces have seldom been produced by a pioneer," he cautions, emphasizing that "Margaret Cavendish was one of the first English women seriously to undertake written composition."[262] Perry devotes an entire chapter to her "minor writings," including an overview of her "poems and pseudo-science," an extended analysis of *The World's Olio* and *Nature's Pictures*, and a detailed examination of her plays. Perry sees in her drama the "limitless scope" of her "fancy," even though he regards her "dramatic technique" as "completely lacking." While noting that her plays could not be acted when they were published, he also points out that "time went on and conditions changed," but that her plays

---

[261] In 1919 Henry E. Huntington established the Huntington Library in San Marino, California. The Library owns a significant number of original Cavendish works in its rare books collection; the library's catalogue is at http://catalog.huntington.org/#.

[262] Perry, *The First Duchess of Newcastle*, 171.

"remained unacted and unactable." Her drama is "lifeless" and "so dull that one shrinks from it even on the printed page"; her plays represent the "lowest ebb" of Cavendish's literary output. Nevertheless, Perry manfully works through all of them, producing summaries and brief analyses for every play included in Cavendish's two folio collections. This chapter on her minor writings concludes with a discussion of her orations, the *Sociable Letters*, and *The Blazing World* and is followed next by a chapter about "The Duchess Herself."[263] After all this careful reading and effort, the best Perry can muster in the end is this assessment: if Cavendish and her husband were not "of supreme moment" as "producers of literature," they were at least "individual and attractive personages."

Such was the state of affairs when Virginia Woolf came to write about Margaret Cavendish, condemning her as some kind of kudzu-like vine, strangling everything and anything in her pathway. The three progressively more sympathetic full-length biographies produced in the late twentieth and early twenty-first centuries—Douglas Grant's *Margaret the First* (1957), Kathleen Jones's *A Glorious Fame* (1988), and Katie Whitaker's *Mad Madge* (2002)—provide correctives to the apocryphal stories about Cavendish without sacrificing any of the pleasures of juicy gossip or the occasional absurdities of Cavendish's life. And it has been the work of a generation of feminist scholars to vault Margaret Cavendish right into the canon of British literature, where we find her comfortably established today.

A Note on the Text

This edition of *The Female Academy* began with my transcription from a British Library copy of the 1662 *Playes*.[264] In preparing this edition, I have also relied on the copy of *Playes* available at the Early English

---

[263] The minor writings are covered in Perry, *The First Duchess of Newcastle*, Chapter 3 (pp. 171-264); the following chapter (pp. 265-313) is on Cavendish's life, focusing primarily on her autobiography, but Perry also includes Margaret Cavendish's love letters to her husband, as transcribed and printed by Richard William Goulding, ed., *Letters of Margaret Lucas to Her Future Husband* (London: John Murray, 1909).

[264] The British Library owns three copies of Cavendish's 1662 *Playes*, including the one I refer to here, General Reference Collection 79.I.14.

Books Online (EEBO) database. In this way, a reader who is interested in looking at the original play, as published by Cavendish, can access and read *The Female Academy* in the original alongside the carefully edited version in the pages that follow in this volume.

Even for those who feel comfortable reading seventeenth-century English prose, Cavendish presents some obstacles. In a note prefacing her edition of several of Cavendish's plays, Anne Shaver writes that she has "retained Cavendish's eccentric spelling, grammar, and punctuation because these are aspects of her works that have occasioned comment from the moment they appeared."[265] About these "eccentric" aspects of Cavendish's texts, Kate Lilley notes that, while "Cavendish's extremely idiosyncratic punctuation and grammar have usually been seen as simply a function of her lack of formal education and carelessness in overseeing the preparation of her manuscripts," something more than "carelessness" is also at work: "It seems to me important not to discount the defiance with which Cavendish treated normative writing practices at every level." She seems not only to have recognized "the transgressive potential of grammatical singularity" but to have exploited it.[266]

Cavendish herself well aware of the problems in her published work. In an "Epistle to the Reader" included in *The World's Olio*, she acknowledges that her book is "not so well done" as it could be: "a little more care might have placed the words so as the language might have run smoother," she writes, but since she is "of a lazy disposition," she has decided to "let it go into the world with its defects rather than take the pains to refine it."[267] Later in the same book, she comes back to the subject of the "defects" in her writing. About her grammar, she admits that she is "no scholar, and therefore understand[s] it not," but still, she is compelled to add, "that little I have heard of it is enough for me to renounce it, for if I have any wit, it is so little that it would be lost in scholastical rules." Besides, "it were worse to be a pedantic woman than a pedantic man."[268] And yet, despite this brave defiance, she knows that

---

[265] Margaret Cavendish, *The Convent of Pleasure and Other Plays*, ed. Anne Shaver (Baltimore: Johns Hopkins University Press, 1999), xi.

[266] Lilley, ed., *The Blazing World and Other Writings*, xxxiii.

[267] Cavendish, "An Epistle to the Reader," *The Worlds Olio*, n. p. (precedes Book 1). I have silently modernized the spelling and punctuation.

[268] Cavendish, "The Epistle," *The Worlds Olio*, n. p. (precedes Book 2). I have silently modernized the spelling and punctuation.

she lives "in a carping age" where "some find fault with my former writings because they are not grammar nor good orthography." She blames her printer for her bad spelling, claiming he should have "rectified" it, because it is "against nature for a woman to spell right," confessing that she "cannot."

She takes a similarly contradictory stance in presenting her first volume of plays to her reader. By this point she has acquired a new printer, but despite the change, the texts found in the 1662 *Plays* are filled with all kinds of grammatical, spelling, and punctuation errors.[269] An *errata* page follows her final epistle to her readers, but after a dense paragraph listing various corrections, there is a note indicating that these are just "the most considerable errors of the press" affecting sense or meaning. There are many errors remaining, "obvious to the eyes": "misspellings, omissions, misplacing of letters, syllables, and sometimes words." But these are "too numerous to be here set down" and in any case they are "so inconsiderable that they may be by every common reader at once observed and corrected."

Whether or not a "common reader" might overlook all of these "inconsiderable errors," as Cavendish argues, I have silently corrected the mechanical errors in the edition that follows. With the aim of presenting a more readable text for those unfamiliar with the peculiarities of seventeenth-century printed books (not to mention Cavendish's "eccentricities"), I have modernized the spelling and capitalization throughout. Punctuation presents a more complicated set of problems. As is the norm in the period, the commas, semi-colons, colons, and periods are used more rhetorically, as a guide to reading, than grammatically, following the kind of systematic rules we find today in a handbook like Diana Hacker's *A Writer's Reference*. My aim has been to bring the punctuation more into conformity with twenty-first century norms without erasing completely the texture and flavor of the original.

Cavendish's grammar presents a more difficult set of questions. I have not "corrected" many of the obvious grammatical errors in *The Female Academy*, for example the overwhelming number of problems with subject-verb agreement. If Cavendish's grammar is so confused as to obscure her meaning, I have emended lightly or provided a reading in

---

[269] On Cavendish's publishers, see below, "A Brief Chronology of Margaret Cavendish's Published Work," 165-68.

the notes, but otherwise I have thought it best to let Cavendish "renounce" the "scholastical rules." I have also retained Cavendish's original paragraphing throughout, although this frequently means a reader faces a substantial block of prose.

As an aid to readers, I have footnoted words and phrases where definitions, clarifications, and explanations might be helpful. When the meaning of a word is complicated or difficult, or where the meaning of the word has changed significantly from Cavendish's time, I have quoted relevant definitions from the *Oxford English Dictionary*.

The layout and format of the play's text have also been carefully considered for the modern reader. Cavendish has divided *The Female Academy* into five acts, but the scenes are numbered consecutively throughout the play; while this is not the way modern play texts present acts and scenes, I have retained Cavendish's system of numbering here so that readers consulting critical essays on *The Female Academy* will not face confusion. In the play, all stage directions are set in italic type, a font that has been retained here. Character names in the speech headings are italicized and sometimes abbreviated in the original, but they have been written in full and set in capital letters in this edition. Proper nouns, but not titles, are also set in italics in the original (for example "Lady *Wit*"); these italics have not been retained.

The Female Academy

The Actors' Names[1]

Two grave matrons belonging to the Female Academy
Two or three ancient ladies
Two or three citizens' wives
A company of young gentlemen and others

---

[1] The play's list of *dramatis personae* is notably incomplete. Most obviously, it doesn't include the "company of young ladies" inside the Female Academy, several of whom function as the "lady speakers" addressing their peers in the lengthy "discourses" that make up the scenes inside the academy. The list also fails to include two gentlewomen who are not enclosed within the Female Academy and whose conversation makes up an entire scene (2.7) and a manservant who speaks in the final scene of the play. In this list, Cavendish also indicates that there are "two or three" elderly gentlewomen in the play, though there are three, all of whom have speaking roles (3.15); similarly, the list indicates there are "two or three citizens' wives" in the play though, again, there are specifically three, all of whom have speaking rolls (2.11). While Cavendish notes that there is "a company" of "young gentlemen" in the play, six young gentlemen have speaking roles in one scene (5.25). It's not clear who is meant by the "and others" following the "company" of young gentlemen in her list of the play's characters.

ACT 1, Scene 1

Enter two ancient ladies.

FIRST LADY. If you would have your daughter virtuously and wisely educated, you must put her into the Female Academy.

SECOND LADY. The Female Academy? What is that?

FIRST LADY. Why, a house wherein a company of young ladies are instructed by old matrons[2] as to speak wittily and rationally and to behave themselves handsomely and to live virtuously.

SECOND LADY. Do any men come amongst them?

FIRST LADY. Oh, no, only there is a large, open grate[3] whereon[4] the outside men stand, which come to hear and see them, but no men enter into the academy nor women but those that are put in for

---

[2] The word *matron* not only refers to a married woman of "mature" years but also connotes a woman with "dignity, propriety, and moral or social rank" (*Oxford English Dictionary* [online], www.oed.com, hereafter cited as *OED*). The ladies speaking here are described in the stage directions as *ancient*, which also identifies them as mature, if not elderly, women.

[3] A *grate* is a barred window or opening that will allow some communication between the women inside the Female Academy and the outside world, but the bars prevent the young women from leaving—or escaping—and they will prevent any unauthorized person—in particular the "outside men"—from entering.

Although the Female Academy is a secular rather than a religious institution, the young men in this play (2.6) somehow assume that the women have "encloistered" themselves, suggesting that the men regard the academy as the equivalent of a convent. This detail of the grate certainly adds to the young men's conclusion. Notably, while cloistered nuns are not allowed to leave the convent in which they have been enclosed, a regular feature of convent architecture is a grate or grill that allows the women inside to communicate with those outside the institution. Within a convent church, for example, the nuns may hear the mass and take communion from behind a grate, while lay communities might also gather to hear nuns' singing from behind their convent grates. The grate also maintains a separation between the nuns and any lay visitors to the convent parlor while still allowing for communication between a nun and her visitors.

[4] Rather than standing "on" the grate, the lady speaker's description of the men suggests that they gather around the grate, the preposition *whereon* used to mean "close to, beside, near, or just by" (*OED*).

education, for they have another large, open grate at the other end of the room they discourse in, whereon the outside of that grate stand women that come to hear them discourse.

SECOND LADY. I will put my daughter therein to be instructed.

FIRST LADY. If your daughter were not of honorable birth, they would not receive her, for they take in none but those of ancient descent, as also rich, for it is a place of charges.[5]

SECOND LADY. Why, then, they will not refuse my daughter, for she is both honorably born and also rich.

Exeunt.[6]

ACT 1, Scene 2[7]

Enter a company of young ladies and with them two grave matrons,[8] where through the hanging a company of men look on them, as through a grate.[9]

FIRST MATRON. Come, lady, 'tis your turn this day to take the chair.

All sit, and she that speaks sits in an adorned[10] chair.

LADY SPEAKER. Deliver your theme.

---

[5] It is an expensive place.

[6] Literally "they go out" (from the Latin *exire*, "to go out"), a stage direction indicating that all the actors leave the stage.

[7] The act number appears only in the first scene of each act in the play. For ease of reference, the act number has been added at the beginning of each scene.

[8] A *matron* is usually thought of as a mature married woman (see n. 1, above), but the word can also refer to a "woman in charge of the domestic arrangements" of an institution, like a school or hospital" (*OED*).

[9] Cavendish's stage directions for this scene suggest something of the way she envisions it being performed, with a *hanging*—a piece of cloth or drapery—used to depict the Female Academy's grate separating the young women inside the academy from the young men outside.

[10] A chair somehow decorated or "embellished" to "confer distinction" (*OED*).

FIRST MATRON. You speak, lady, like a robber when he says, "Deliver your purse," but you must say, "Propound[11] your theme."

LADY SPEAKER. Why, then, propound your theme.

FIRST MATRON. I present to your opinion whether women are capable to have as much wit or wisdom as men.

LADY SPEAKER. First, I must define what wit and wisdom are: as for Wit, it is the daughter of Nature,[12] and Wisdom is a son of the gods. This daughter of Nature, the Lady Wit, is very beautiful, and for the most part her countenance is very amiable and her speech delightful; in her accouterments,[13] she is as all other of the female sex are, various, as sometimes in plain garments and sometimes in glittering[14] garments and sometimes she is attired in garments of as many several colors as the rainbow, and she alters in their fashions as often as in their substances or trimmings. As for her humor,[15] it is according to the nature of her sex, which is as various and changing as her accouterments, for that sometimes she is merry and jesting, other

---

[11] "To put forward, set forth, propose, or offer for consideration, discussion, acceptance, or adoption; to put forward as a question for solution" (*OED*).

[12] Cavendish incorporates the story of Lady Nature and her daughters in a two-part play earlier in the 1662 collection, *Natures Three Daughters, Beauty, Love, and Wit* (Part 1, 491-508; Part 2, 509-26). In the first part of the play, Mademoiselle Tell-Truth observes that "the Lady Natures Daughters are the only Ladies that are admired, praised, adored, worshiped, and sued to & all other women are despised" (1.1). While Beauty and Love are somewhat "retired" and difficult to see, Lady Wit "doth discourse often in public" (1.3). Much like the young women speakers in *The Female Academy*, Lady Wit delivers several extended speeches before an audience in the play (Part 1, 2.7, 4.13; Part 2, 1.1, 3.13, 5.20).

While it is quite clear here that Nature is personified, elsewhere in *The Female Academy* it is not always so obvious. In the scenes that follow, when Cavendish refers to Nature as a person, the word has been capitalized; otherwise—when nature is a referred to as a concept or force—the word has not been capitalized.

[13] Clothing or dress.

[14] While *glittering* can mean "sparkly," here it seems to be used as the opposite of *plain*, and so probably means "showy or splendid" (*OED*).

[15] The word *humor* derives from ancient and medieval medical theory that relates the four bodily fluids or "humors" (from the late Latin *humor*, meaning "moisture" or "fluid")—blood, phlegm, yellow bile, and black bile—to a range of psychological types and characteristics (*OED*).

times pleasing and delightful, sometimes melancholy, sometimes fantastical, other times spiteful and censorious, and oft times wild and wanton unless Discretion rules and leads her, who[16] keeps her within the bounds and pales of modesty. Also her discourses are various, as sometimes she will flatter grossly, other times she will rail maliciously, and sometimes she will speak so eloquently and demean[17] herself so elegantly as to ravish the minds of the beholders and hearers. This Lady Wit hath nine daughters, very beautiful ladies, namely the nine Muses,[18] and every several Muse partakes of every several humor of the mother. These nine beautiful ladies, Nature's grandchildren and Wit's daughters, have vowed single lives, living always in the court with their mother, whose court is a very glorious palace, for it is composed of celestial flame, and divine spirits were the architectures[19] thereof. The servants and courtiers of the Lady Wit are poets, men of all nations, qualities, dignities, and humors. These courtiers, the poets, make love to the Lady Wit's daughters, the nine muses, and often receive favors from them, which favors their servants, the poets, braid them into rhymes and make several works of verse, then tie them into true lovers' knots[20] and then, as all lovers used to do with their mistress's favors, vaingloriously show them to the public view of the world, for though the lady muses will not marry, yet they receive courtly addresses and take delight to be wooed and sued to. The younger sort of poets are amorous[21] lovers, the grave and more ancient poets are platonic lovers and some are divine lovers and some are

---

[16] The relative pronoun *who* refers here to *Discretion*, personified in the same way as Nature and Wit.

[17] "To conduct, carry on" (*OED*).

[18] In classical mythology, the nine Muses are goddesses who preside over learning and arts, including music and poetry. According to classical mythology, the Muses were the daughters of Zeus and Mnemosyne, the goddess of memory (whose mother was Gaia, the primal Mother Earth).

[19] For "architects."

[20] "A kind of ornamental knot (often either a double-looped bow, or a knot formed of two loops intertwined) used as a symbol of true love" (*OED*).

[21] The word *amorous* is generally regarded as meaning, simply, someone who is "inclined to love" or "fond of the opposite sex" and is thus used to describe someone who is loving or maybe even ardent, perhaps the meaning intended here, but the word as used by Cavendish later in the play (5.28) has a decidedly negative connotation, with *amorous* referring to a "corrupt" or "filthy" sexual desire (a meaning also supported by the *OED*).

heroic lovers and some are satirical lovers, which woo in a crabbed[22] style. But to conclude of Wit, there are good wits which have foolish judgments, for though Wit and Wisdom are sisters and brothers, both the children of Nature, yet for the most part the brother is a mere fool[23] and the sister hath a great wit, but some have masculine wits and effeminate judgments, as if their beams were hermaphrodite.[24]

The next I am to define is Wisdom, who, as I said, is a son of the gods. This Wisdom is a person of perfect and upright shape, of well-composed features, of a manly garb and an assured countenance. In his speech he is of a ready delivery, and he hath a well-tempered humor. As for the accouterments of his person, he changes them according to the times and occasions. His constant habitation is in the strong tower of Honesty; this tower is built round, without ends or corners or by-places,[25] and it stands upon four pillars, as prudence, fortitude, justice, and temperance. Upon every several pillar are letters engraved wherein may be read the proper uses, benefits, and advantages of each pillar. These pillars of support cause this tower to be impregnable, for though there are many assaults made against it, as by Riches, which shoots his golden bullets out of his golden cannons at it, striving to batter it down, and Power brings a mighty army to assault it, and Danger of Death strives to storm it, and Flattery and Insinuation to undermine it, yet it holds out without any breach therein, for the walls of this tower, named Honesty, are of a wonderful strength, for they are as durable as an entire diamond, not to be dissolved, and as transparent as a crystal, without the least spot, stain, or blemish. In this tower, as I said, lives Wisdom; a most magnificent lord he is and is attended numerously and nobly. His chief favorite is

---

[22] Harsh or disagreeable.

[23] To clarify this confusing assertion, since the Lady Speaker has identified Wit's brother, Wisdom, as "a son of the gods": the speaker explains, below, that what passes for wisdom among most men is not "right and true"—and thus this claim that *for the most the brother is a mere fool.*

[24] From the mythological Hermaphroditus, the son of Hermes and Aphrodite whose body was merged with that of the nymph Salmacis, *hermaphrodite* can refer to having the physical characteristics of both sexes, but it can also mean, more generally, "combining two opposite qualities or attributes" (*OED*). I have silently emended Cavendish's unique spelling, "hermophrica," here.

[25] "A place situated aside, an out-of-the-way spot; an odd corner" (*OED*).

Truth; his chief councilors are Reason, Understanding, Observation, Experience, and Judgment; his chief officers are Patience, Industry, and Opportunity; his domestic servants are the appetites, which servants he rules and governs with great moderation; his nobility are the passions, which he prefers according to their merit, but those that are apt to be factious,[26] he severely punishes, for he is one that loves peace and hates *brouilleries*[27] or any dissension. He is a person of the quickest sense, for he hath a most piercing sight to foresee dangers as to avoid them and can well distinguish the right ways from the wrong; likewise he hath a most clear hearing, for nothing passes by that concerns him, but the sound gives him an alarm to stand upon his guard or a charge to take his advantage, but he hath a silent tongue, for he never speaks but it is to some purpose; also he hath a marvelous quick scent to smell out a rebellion or treason, and he will follow it pace by pace, as hounds do hares, and never leaves till he hath hunted it out. Also his touch is very sensible; he soon feels a courtesy or injury, the first he receives gratefully and feels tenderly, the other he receives strongly and grips hard, when he can take fast hold, otherwise he lets it pass or fall, as if his touch were numbed. He is a person which is so solicited by the weak, sought to by the wronged, flattered by the ambitious, sued to by the distressed, and he often sits in the court of errors to rectify the disorder therein. Sometimes he hath been in great human councils, but that is very rare; indeed he is so seldom in great human councils as he is hardly known, for not one among a thousand that did ever see him, much less to have any acquaintance with him, for he is reserved and not company for everyone. But there are many that falsely pretend not only to be acquainted with him, but gets false vizards[28] and pretend to be Wisdom itself, and the world for the most part is cozened and abused with these cheats in not knowing the right and true Wisdom, and how should they, when Wisdom itself appears so seldom, as he is a stranger even in kings' courts and princes' palaces, and so great a stranger he is in many courts and councils that if by chance he should be there, they thrust him out as a troublesome guest and laugh at his advice as foolish or condemn his council as treacherous. But now I have declared unto you whom Wit and

[26] To engage in dispute or conflict, especially as part of a faction.
[27] Disturbances.
[28] Masks (from the English "visor," derived from the Anglo-French *viser*, "face").

Wisdom are, now I am to give my opinion whether women are capable of their society. But truly I must tell you it is a difficult question, by reason the several[29] educations, which are the ushers that lead human creatures to several societies, for there are societies of the ignorant and foolish as well as of the witty and wise, and several ushers belonging thereto. And indeed these latter societies are numerous and of all sorts; the other are societies of the most choicest, for though Wit is not an absolute goddess nor human Wisdom an absolute god, yet they are a degree[30] above other earthly mortals, but fools are produced from the degrees of mortality, and Ignorance is the daughter of Obscurity. The ushers o[f] these are Obstinacy, Stupidity, and Illiterature,[31] which leads mortals to dangerous and inaccessible ways. In this last society, for the most part women are of, as being bred therein, and having such ill tutors and guides, they must needs err, for there is an old saying, "When the blind leads the blind, they must needs fall into the ditch,"[32] not having sight to choose their way. So women breeding up women, the generations must needs be fools, for the first wom[a]n[33] had an ill tutor, the devil, which neither instructed her in the knowledge of wisdom nor wit but learned[34] her hurtful dissimulation, to which she hath bred all her female generations successively, as from female to female. But your question is whether women are capable of wit and wisdom. Truly, in my opinion, women are more capable of wit than wisdom, by reason they are both of the female gender, which may cause some sympathy in their natures, and in some things they do plainly sympathy and agree, for Wit is wild and various, and so are women, and Wit is busy and meddles with every thing, cause, or subject, so do women; Wit is fantastical and so are women, Wit is always in extremes and so are women, Wit doth talk

---

[29] Distinct or particular.

[30] Here *degree* refers to a "step" in a "direct line of descent," either "upward or downward" (*OED*).

[31] "Want of learning; illiterateness, illiteracy" (*OED*).

[32] "Let them alone: they be blinde leaders of the blinde. And if the blinde lead the blinde, both shall fall into the ditch" (Matthew 15:14). From *The Holy Bible: A Facsimile . . . of the Authorized Version Published in the Year 1611* (New York: Oxford University Press, 1911).

[33] Although the text here reads "first wom*e*n," plural, the passage suggests Cavendish is referring to the first wom*a*n, Eve, tempted by Satan in Genesis.

[34] Taught.

much and so do women, Wit is humorsome[35] and so are women, Wit is prodigal and so are women, Wit loves praises and so do women, Wit doth sport and play, dance, and sing the time away, and so do women, Wit is many times wanton and so are women. Thus far are women capable of the society and conversation of Wit, but I doubt of her subtle invention, quick apprehension, rare conceptions, elevated fancy, and smooth elocution.

As for Wisdom, women seem to all outward appearance to have a natural antipathy, abhorring his severe and strict rules, hating his medicable[36] admonitions, his profitable counsels and advice, his wary ways, his prudent forecast, his serious actions, his temperate life and sober disposition, all which makes them incapable[37] of the society of Wisdom.

Exeunt.

ACT 2, Scene 3[38]

Enter two gentlemen.

FIRST GENTLEMAN. I suppose you have heard that a company of young gentlemen have set up an academy next to the ladies' academy.

SECOND GENTLEMAN. We heard nothing of it.

FIRST GENTLEMAN. Why, then, I will tell you: the men are very angry that the women should speak so much and they so little, I think, for they have made that room which they stood in to see and hear the ladies speak

---

[35] "Subject to moods or humours; whimsical, capricious; peevish, ill-humoured" (*OED*).

[36] Medicinal.

[37] "Unable or unfit to receive so as to be affected or influenced by; not open to or susceptible of; unable to 'take in' so as to realize, insensible to" (*OED*).

[38] Although *The Female Academy* is divided into five acts, the scenes are numbered consecutively throughout the entire play. For ease of reference, I have retained Cavendish's consecutive scene numbers.

into a place for themselves to speak in that the ladies may hear what they can say.

SECOND GENTLEMAN. Faith,[39] if you will have my opinion, it is that the men do it out of a mockery to the ladies.

FIRST GENTLEMAN. 'Tis likely so, for they rail extremely that so many fair young ladies are so strictly enclosed as not to suffer men to visit them in the academy.

SECOND GENTLEMAN. Faith, if the men should be admitted into their academy, there would be work enough for the grave matrons were it but to act the part of midwives.[40]

Exeunt.

ACT 2, Scene 4

Enter the academy ladies and their grave matrons. Another of the young ladies sits as lady speaker in an armed chair, the rest on stools about her.

MATRON. Lady, at this time let the theme of your discourse be of discour[s]ing.[41]

LADY SPEAKER. As for discourse, it is differently various; some discourses are delightful and pleasing, others tedious and troublesome, some rude and uncivil, some vain and unnecessary, some graceful and acceptable, some wise and profitable, but in most discourses time is lost, having nothing that is worthy to be learned, practiced, or observed. But there are two sorts of discourses or manner of ways of discoursings, as there is a discoursing within the mind and a discourse with words. As for the inward discourse in the mind, it is to discourse to a man's self, as if they were discoursing to others, making questions or propositions,

---

[39] From "in faith," a mild interjection meaning "truly" or "really."

[40] The second gentleman "jokes" that if the young men were somehow to find their way into the all-female academy, the young women would all become pregnant.

[41] Cavendish includes many brief reflections on discourse and "discoursing" in *The Worlds Olio*, some of which parallel the points her lady speaker makes here.

syllogisms, and conclusions to himself, wherein a man may deceive himself with his own false arguments, for it is an old saying that it is one thing to oppose himself and another thing to be opposed by others, and it is easy to argue without opposition.[42] As for discoursing with words, it is more difficult than to discourse with thoughts, for though words are as high and substantial as thoughts, yet the mouth is not so ready in speaking as the brain in thinking, and the brain can present more thoughts at one time than the mouth can deliver words at one time. But words, or rhetoric, is apt to deceive a man as his conceptions, especially orators, which draw themselves with the force of rhetoric from the right and the truth, so as an orator is as apt to delude himself as to delude his auditory[43] if he make words or eloquence the ground of his questions, persuasions, or judgment and not reason, for reason must find out the truth and right, and truth must judge the cause. But rhetoric is for the most part a vizard to right reason, for it seems a natural face and is not so: rhetoric seems right reason but is not. Also there are extemporal[44] discourses and discourses premeditated; extemporal sounds best to the ears of the hearers although of less wit than premeditated discourses because they are delivered more naturally and so flow more freely and easily, which makes the noise not only to sound more sweetly but the discourse to be more delightful both to the ears and the mind of the hearers and more ready to the understanding. But of all discourses, the disputive[45] discourses are harshest; indeed, all disputive discourses are

---

[42] Unidentified. Although the speaker implies that she is referring to a recognized proverb ("it is an old saying") or perhaps, as above (n. 32), that she is quoting from the Bible, this "old saying" is not marked out by italics in the text as the earlier one had been. This "saying" does not appear in a contemporary source like John Ray's *A Collection of English Proverbs, Digested into a convenient Method for the speedy finding any one upon occasion* . . . (London, 1670), nor is it included in modern collections of proverbs, like Morris Palmer Tilley's *A Dictionary of the Proverbs in England in the Sixteenth and Seventeenth Centuries* . . . (Ann Arbor: University of Michigan Press, 1950). The closest biblical parallel seems to be from 1 Corinthians 3:18: "Let no man deceive himself: If any man among you seemeth to bee wise in this world, let him become a foole, that he may be wise" (*The Holy Bible: A Facsimile . . . of the Authorized Version Published in the Year 1611*).

[43] Audience.

[44] "Done, said, or conceived on the spur of the moment; not premeditated or studied beforehand; impromptu; off-hand" (*OED*).

[45] Disputative.

like chromatic[46] music, wherein is more skill than harmony. But all discourses should be fitted, measured, or chosen to the time, place, persons, and occasions, for that discourse which is proper for one time, place, or person is improper for another time, place, or person, as a discourse of mirth in a time of sadness, a familiar discourse from an inferior to a superior, a vain discourse to a serious humor or an effeminate discourse to a man or a masculine discourse to a woman, and many the like examples might be given. Also there are discourses that are sensible discourses, rational discourses, and witty discourses. Also there are other discourses that have neither sense, reason, wit, nor fancy in them. Also there are clownish discourses and courtly discourses. Also there is a general discoursing and particular discoursing, also scholastical discourses and poetical discourses. But of all the several ways, manners, or sorts of discourses and discoursings, let me commend the poetical discourses and discoursings, which are brief and quick, full of variety, curiosity, and newness, being as new as peep of day, as refreshing as the zephyrus[47] wind, as modest as the blushing morning, sweet as the flowery spring, as pleasant as a summer's evening, as profitable as autumn's harvest, as splendorous as the midday sun, as flowing as the full tide sea, as dilating as the spreading air, as fruitful as the fertile earth, and have as great an influence upon the natures, dispositions, and humors of men as the stars and planets in the heavens have; it takes life from the celestial flame and is produced from the gods on high, and this discourse makes man resemble to a deity.

Exeunt.

ACT 2, Scene 5

Enter two gentlemen as meeting each other.

FIRST GENTLEMAN. Whither so hastily?

---

[46] In music, *chromatic* tones "are the notes in a composition that are outside the seven-note diatonic (i.e., major and minor) scales and tones" (*Encyclopedia Britannica Online* [online], s.v. "Chromaticism").

[47] "A soft mild gentle wind or breeze" (*OED*), from Zephyrus, Greek god of the west wind.

SECOND GENTLEMAN. I am going to hear them speak in the academy.

FIRST GENTLEMAN. They have done for this time.

SECOND GENTLEMAN. And did they speak well?

FIRST GENTLEMAN. As they use to do.[48]

SECOND GENTLEMAN. Why, they never spake[49] before there!

FIRST GENTLEMAN. Where?

SECOND GENTLEMAN. Why, in the academy.

FIRST GENTLEMAN. Why, I am sure I heard one lady speak yesterday and another to day.

SECOND GENTLEMAN. Ladies? I mean the Academy of Men.

FIRST GENTLEMAN. Why, do the men intend to speak?

SECOND GENTLEMAN. Yes, presently, if they have not done speaking already.

Exeunt.

ACT 2, Scene 6

Enter a company of young men, as in the room next to the ladies. One takes the chair.

GENTLEMAN SPEAKER. Gentlemen, we need no learned scholars nor grave sages to propound the theme of our discourse in this place and at this time, for our minds are so full of thoughts of the female sex as we have no room for any other subject or object. Wherefore, let the theme

---

[48] As they usually do.
[49] Spoke (*spake* is an archaic form of the simple past tense of the verb "speak").

be what it will, our discourses will soon run on them, but if we could bring women as easily into our arms as into our brains, and had we as many mistresses in our possessions as we have in our imaginations, we should be much more happy than we are. Nay, had we been blind, deaf, and insensible to the sex, we had been happy, unless that sex had been more kinder than they are, but they are cruel, which makes men miserable. But Nature had made beauty in vain, if not for the use of the masculine sex, wherefore Nature forbids restraint, and 'tis a sin against Nature for women to be encloistered, retired, or restrained. Nay, it is not only a sin against Nature, but a grievous sin against the gods for women to live single lives or to vow virginity, for if women live virgins, there will be no saints for heaven nor worship nor adoration offered to the gods from earth, for if all women live virgins, the race of mankind will be utterly extinguished, and if it be a general sin to live virgins, no particular can be exempted, and if it be lawful for one to live a virgin, it is lawful for all, so if it be unlawful for one, it is unlawful for all, but surely the gods would not make anything lawful that were against themselves. But to conclude, those women which restrain themselves from the company and use of men are damned, being accused by men, judged by Nature, and condemned by the gods.

Exeunt.

ACT 2, Scene 7

Enter two gentlewomen.

FIRST GENTLEWOMAN. What say you? Will you go into the academy?

SECOND GENTLEWOMAN. No, faith, I mean not to be damned.

FIRST GENTLEWOMAN. I am of your mind. I will run unto the men to save me.

SECOND GENTLEWOMAN. So will I, since the ways of salvation are so easy and so pleasant.

Exeunt.

ACT 2, Scene 8

Enter the academy of ladies and the grave matroness.[50] *The lady that is to speak takes a chair.*

MATRON. Lady, let the theme of your discourse be at this time on the behavior of our sex.

LADY SPEAKER. It is a greater difficulty for a woman to behave herself discreetly in private visitations than for a man to speak wisely in privy councils, and it is a greater difficulty for a woman to behave herself well in a public assembly than for a man to speak eloquently in a public auditory, and it is a greater difficulty for a woman to behave herself well to several persons and in several assemblies than for a man to behave himself gallantly in several battles, and as much dishonor comes in the misbehavior of the one as the cowardliness of the other. Wherefore there requires as much skill, care, and conduct in a woman's behavior in visiting, entertaining, placing, applying, and discoursing, as to a commander in mustering, training, entrenching, besieging, embattling, fighting, and retreating, for it is not enough for a woman to behave herself according to her degree, quality, dignity, birth and breeding,[51] age, beauty, wit, and fortune, but according to time, place and occasion, business, and affairs, as also to the humors, capacities, professions, dignities, qualities, births, breedings, fortunes, ages, and sexes of those persons she is in company and conversation withal.[52] Also in mixed companies she must have a mixed behavior and mixed discourses, as sometimes to one, then to another, according as she can handsomely and civilly apply or address herself and to those that apply and address themselves to her, for a woman must not behave herself or discourse unto a great lord or prince as to a peasant or to a peasant as to a great

---

[50] The *OED* records no examples of the word *matroness* (or, as Cavendish spells it here, "matronnesse"). Cavendish presumably creates the word to parallel "patroness" or "baroness" (or, as in 2.10, below, *conqueresse*), but since the word *matron* already denotes a woman, the *–ess* suffix is superfluous.

[51] All of these—degree, quality, dignity, birth, and breeding—are roughly synonymous terms, emphasizing the concern for rank (or position), especially of high rank, in society.

[52] The preposition *withal* is substituted here in the postposition for "with" (*OED*).

lord or prince, nor to a soldier as to a divine, nor to a divine as to a
soldier, nor to a statesman as to a tradesman, nor to a tradesman as to a
statesman, nor to a flattering gallant as to a grave senior, nor to a grave
senior as to a flattering gallant, nor to a young man as to an ancient man,
nor to a boy as to a man, nor to a woman as to a man, nor to a poet as
to a woman or as to those men that understand not poetry, nor to learned
men as to ignorant men. Also an ancient, grave matron must not behave
herself like a wanton young girl, nor a wife like a maid, nor a widow like
a wife, nor a mother like her daughter, nor a mistress like her servant,
nor a servant like a mistress, nor a great lady like a country wife, nor a
country wife like a great lady, for that would be ridiculous. Indeed it is
easier for a middle rank or degree, at least it is oftener seen, to behave
themselves better than those of high titles and great estates or those of
a very mean condition and of low birth, for the one is apt to err with
excessive pride, the other with an excessive rudeness, both being bold
and ignorantly bred, knowing not how to be civil, nor what belongs to
civil persons, for the pride of the one scorns to be instructed, and the
poverty of the other hath not means to keep and pay instructors, for the
excess of plenty nuzzles[53] the one in ignorance, and excess of poverty
blindfolds the other from knowledge. But to conclude of the behavior
of women, first as to the generality, they must behave themselves civilly
and circumspectly, to particulars, modestly and friendly, for the chief
principles of behavior are twelve, six good and six bad. The six good are
ceremony, civility, modesty, humility, friendship, and obedience: the first
is majestical and magnificent; the second, noble; the third, virtuous; the
fourth, humane; the fifth, generous; the sixth, pious. The first is graceful;
the second, sociable; the third, delightful; the fourth, natural; the fifth,
helpful; the sixth, necessary. The first belongs to dignity, the second to
breeding, the third to youth, the fourth to age, the fifth to wealth, the
sixth to peace.

As for the six bad principles, [they are] to be proud, bold, rude, wanton,
disobedient, and cruel: the first is insolent; the second, impudent; the
third, ignorant; the fourth, brutish; the fifth, unnatural; the sixth, wicked.
The first lives with mean births joined with good fortune, the second
lives with ignorant and doltish spirits, the third with base breeding, the

---

[53] Trains or nurtures.

fourth with beasts, the fifth with uncivil nations, the sixth with atheists. The first is to be slighted, the second to be pitied, the third to be shunned, the fourth to be hated, the fifth to be governed, the sixth to be punished.

Exeunt.

ACT 2, Scene 9

Enter two gentlemen.

FIRST GENTLEMAN. What say you to these young ladies?

SECOND GENTLEMAN. I say that, though they be but young ladies, they discourse like old women.

Exeunt.

ACT 2, Scene 10

Enter a company of young gentlemen. The gentleman speaker takes the chair.

GENTLEMAN SPEAKER. The beauty of the female sex hath as great an influence upon the eyes of men as the stars of the heavens have upon their nature and disposition, but as a cloud of ill education covers, changes, or buries the good influence of the stars, so a cloud of time covers, changes, and buries the beauties of the fairest ladies' faces, which alters the affections of men and buries all the delight that was received therefrom in the ruins of age and the graves of wrinkles. But beauty, whilst it is fresh and flourishing, it is the most powerful conqueress and triumphs in the chariot of youth, and though her masculine subjects forsake her when time hath displaced her and weakened her power, yet she were unwise not to take pleasure in her victories whilst she may.

Exeunt.

ACT 2, Scene 11

Enter two citizens' wives.[54]

FIRST WIFE. Come, come, neighbor, we shall get no room to see and hear the young ladies if we go not quickly.

SECOND WIFE. Yes, let us go; but stay, neighbor, I must run home again, for I have left the key in the cellar door.

FIRST WIFE. Let it be there for this time.

SECOND WIFE. By my truth,[55] I must not, for my maid Joan and the apprentice will drink out all my ale and strong beer, and there will be none left to give my husband a draught when he goeth to bed.

Enter another citizen's wife.

FIRST WIFE. What, neighbor, are you come back already?

THIRD WIFE. Why, there is no getting in. The doorkeeper beat me back and said there was no room for citizens' wives, for the room was only kept for ladies and gentlewomen of quality.[56]

SECOND WIFE. Well, we may come to be ladies one day, although not gentlewomen,[57] and then we shall not so often be beaten back.

---

[54] The word *citizen* here is a statement of class: an "ordinary (city- or town-dwelling) person as opposed to a member of the landed nobility or gentry on one hand or an artisan, labourer, etc., on the other" (*OED*).

[55] The phrase is used as an interjection to mean "really" or "truly."

[56] The exclusive nature of the Female Academy was made clear at the outset of the play—as the two ladies in 1.1 note, the Academy accepts "none but those of ancient descent, as also rich, for it is a place of charges."

[57] The second wife draws a distinction here between the *lady*, in its more general sense of the "female head of a household" who has authority over all members of the household, including servants and attendants—and who can thus "behave in a superior manner"—and the *gentlewoman*, a "woman of good birth or breeding," a woman of high social position (*OED*).

FIRST WIFE. Let us go to the gentlemen's side. They will receive us and use us kindly.

Exeunt.

ACT 2, Scene 12

Enter the academy of young ladies and their matrons. They all sit, and the lady speaker takes the chair.

MATRON. Ladies, let the theme of our discourse at this time be of truth.

LADY SPEAKER. Truth, although she hath but one face, which is a natural face, yet she hath many several countenances, for sometimes her countenance is severe, other times kind and familiar, sometimes it is sad, sometimes merry, other times pleasing and delightful. Also she hath as different humors as she hath countenances, according to the cause or occasion; likewise, her presence or approach shows the different effects and several causes, or from one cause on several objects or subjects as, for example, sometimes her approach shows man to be miserable or happy, as when she comes to inform him of good fortune or bad, or when she presents him with right understanding of the condition he is in. But in Truth, in whatsoever countenance or humor she puts on, she is a most beautiful lady, for although she do not shine as the sun, which dazzles and obscures the sight with his splendorous beams, yet she doth appear like a bright, clear day wherein and whereby all things are seen perfectly, and although she have various humors, yet her actions are just, for the alteration of her countenance and humors are not to deceive men, nor she takes no delight in her own sad approach to grieve men, but she doth bear a part, both of their grief and joy. She makes neither the chances, fortunes, accidents, nor actions but only declares[58] them; she is neither the cause nor effects, but only shows the several effects of causes or what causes those effects. She is of a sweet nature and a humble disposition; she doth as freely and commonly accompany the poor as the rich, the mean as the great. Indeed, her constant habitation and dwelling is among the learned and industrious men, but she hath an opposite or

---

[58] Makes them clear or plain.

rival, namely Falsehood, which often obscures her and is often preferred before her. This Falsehood, her rival, is of the nature of a courtesan, as all courtesans are, as to flatter and insinuate herself and company to all men's good liking and good opinion. She is full of deceit and dissembling, and although she hates Truth, yet she imitates her as much as she can; I do not say she imitates the justice, severity, and plainness of Truth, for those, of all things or actions, she shuns, but she imitates her behavior and countenance, for although Falsehood is foul and filthy of herself, yet by artificial paint she makes herself appear as fair and pure as Truth. But the deservingly wise can soon see the difference between the artificial fair of Falsehood and the true, natural, fair complexion of Truth, although fools do admire and are sooner catched,[59] so for the most part deceived with the deceiving arts of Falsehood than the natural verity of Truth, for Falsehood makes a glaring show at the first sight, but the more she is viewed, the worse she appears whereas Truth, the more she is viewed, the better she appears. Also Falsehood uses rhetoric to allure and deceive with her eloquent tongue, whereas Truth speaks little herself but brings always and at all times and in all places and to all things right reason and plain proof to speak for her, who speak without flourishing phrases or decking[60] sentences or scholastical rules, methods, or tenses, but speak to the purpose, deliver the matter briefly, and keep to the sense of truth, or true sense, which is both the best and natural way of speaking and the honest practice of Truth—whereas eloquence is one of the most cozening and abusing arts as is, for as paint is a vizard on the face, so is eloquence a vizard on the mind, and the tongue is the pencil of deceit, drawing the pictures of discourse. Thus Falsehood strives to resemble Truth, as much as artificially she can.

Exeunt.

ACT 3, Scene 13

Enter two gentlemen.

FIRST GENTLEMAN. How do you like the ladies and their discoursings?

---

[59] This form of the past tense of "to catch" was used into the nineteenth century; here *catched* means to be laid hold of or ensnared.

[60] Embellished or ornamented.

SECOND GENTLEMAN. I like some of the ladies' discourses better than others, and I like some of the ladies better than the other, but let us go hear the men.

Exeunt.

ACT 3, Scene 14

Enter a company of gentlemen. He that is to speak takes the chair.

GENTLEMAN SPEAKER. Those women that retire themselves from the company of men are very ungrateful as, first, to Nature, because she made them only for breed. Next to men, who are their defenders, protectors, their nourishers, their maintainers, their instructors, their delighters, their admirers, their lovers and deifiers, as men defend them from the raging, blustering elements by building them houses and not only build them houses for shelter but houses for pleasure and magnificency. Also men protect them from wild, ravenous, and cruel beasts that otherwise would devour them, for as women have not natural strength to build, so have they not natural courage to fight, being for the most part as fearful as weak. Likewise men nourish them, for men fish, fowl,[61] and hunt to get them food to feed them, for which women would neither take the pains nor endure the labor nor have the heart to kill their food, for women by nature are so pitiful and have such tender dispositions as they would rather suffer death themselves than destroy life in other creatures. Also men maintain them by composing themselves into commonwealths wherein is traffic[62] and commerce, that each family may live by each other. Also laws to keep them in peace, to rule them in order, to defend them with arms, which women could never do, by reason they know not what government to settle in or to nor what laws to make, or how to execute those laws that were made; neither could they plead suits, decide causes, judge controversies, deal out right, or punish injuries or condemn criminals.[63] Also men are the instructors to

---

[61] "To catch, hunt, shoot, or snare wildfowl" (*OED*).

[62] "Intercourse, communication; dealings, business" (*OED*).

[63] Contrary to the gentleman speaker's assertion here, at least one woman—Cavendish herself—"creates" a government (in her utopian novel, *The Blazing World*), imagines a woman leading an army (in the two-part *Bell in Campo* [*Playes*, 578-633]), and

inform them of arts and sciences, which women would never have had the patience to study, for they would never have allowed so much time and solitary musing for the perfecting or delivering those conceptions as those that first invented or found them out.[64] Besides, if women were not instructed by men of the natural cause of effects, how often would they have been affrighted almost to death with the loud and terrifying thunders, the flashing lightnings, the dark eclipses, the unsteady earthquakes, the overflowing tides, and many the like natural effects from hidden causes?[65] Besides, women would want all those conveniencies that art affords them and furnishes them with. Also, men instruct women with the mystery of the gods, whereas for want of which knowledge, they would have been damned through ignorance. Also men are their delighters; they traffic on the sea all over the world, to every several climate and country, to find and to bring the female sex curiosities, hazarding their lives for the same, whereas women could neither build their ships nor guide them on the seas when they were built. they have not strength to pull and tug great cable ropes, to set and spread large sails, to cast and weigh massy anchors, no, not in a calm, much less in furious storms with which men often fight, though not with arms, with subtlety and skill, by which the elements are conquered still, whereas women are conquered, and not only being strengthless and heartless, but healthless, for not only the roaring seas and whistling winds and rattling showers and rumbling thunders and fiery lightnings, rocks, shelves, and sands unknown or not to be avoided, besides mountains of ice, if to the northern pole, all which would terrify them, yet their weak bodies, sick stomachs, and nice[66] appetites could never endure long voyages—they would vomit out their life before they could sail to their assigned port or

---

explores political philosophy (in *The Worlds Olio* and *Orations of divers sorts*, for example), including discussions of war and the proper form of government. For a discussion of Cavendish's political philosophy, see *The Stanford Encyclopedia of Philosophy* [online], Winter 2016, s.v. "Margaret Lucas Cavendish," by David Cunning, http://plato.stanford.edu/entries/margaret-cavendish/.

[64] Given the activities of the women in the Female Academy, the gentleman speaker is clearly deluded in his claim that women need men to teach them and that they don't have the "patience" for study.

[65] Again, Cavendish writes a great deal about such natural phenomena, including thunder, winds, storms, and tides, in *The Worlds Olio* and *The Philosophical and Physical Opinions*.

[66] While *nice* can mean careful or particular, it can also mean fussy or finicky, which seems to be more along the gentleman speaker's point.

haven. Also, men are women's admirers, they gaze on their beauties and praise their sweet graces, whereas women through envy detract from each other. Also men are women's only true lovers; they flatter, kiss, and please them, whereas women are apt to quarrel, rail and fight with each other. And lastly, men deify women, making them goddesses by their poetical descriptions and elevations, whereas Nature made them mere mortals, human creatures. Wherefore it is a great ingratitude, nay a horrid ingratitude, in those women that deny men their company, conversation, and communication; wherefore men have not only reason to take it ill, but to be angry with those women that shun or restrain their company from them. But good counsel ought to go before anger, for the difference betwixt good counsel and anger is that good counsel goes before a fault is committed, and anger followeth when a fault is committed, for as good counsel or admonishment is to prevent a fault, so anger is a punishment for a fault past.

Exeunt.

ACT 3, Scene 15

Enter three ancient ladies.

FIRST LADY. Is your daughter put into the academy?

SECOND LADY. Yes.

THIRD LADY. How long, madam, hath your daughter been in the academy?

SECOND LADY. This week, but she hath not profited much, for I do not hear her discourse.

FIRST LADY. First it is to be considered whether your daughter be capable of discoursing, for she must have a natural ingenuity to the art of rhetoric.

THIRD LADY. My daughter was always a pretty talking girl as any in all the country and town I lived in.[67]

SECOND LADY. Yes, children may talk prettily for children, but when they come to be women, it is a question whether they will talk wisely or no. But let us go hear which of the ladies discourses today.

Exeunt.

ACT 3, Scene 16

Enter the academical ladies and their matrons. The lady speaker takes the chair.

MATRON. Lady, for this time let the theme of your discourse be of discourse.[68]

LADY SPEAKER. Reverend matron, this theme hath been discoursed of before by one of our academy, but yet by reason[69] one and the same theme may be discoursed of after different manners or ways, I shall obey you.

As for discourse, there is of four sorts: the first is discoursing in the mind, which is reasoning.

The second is discoursing with words, which is speaking.

The third is discoursing by signs, which is action or acting.

The last is discoursing by figures, which is by letters and hieroglyphics, which is by printing, writing, painting, and the like.

---

[67] Or, more simply, "as pretty a talking girl as."

[68] As the lady speaker quickly notes, the theme of discourse has already been undertaken by one of the Academy's lady speakers (2.4), but it is a topic Cavendish seems to enjoy. Like the young lady here, who notes that "the same theme may be discoursed of after different manners or ways," Cavendish included several reflections on the subject, including "What Discourses Are Enemies to Society," "The Best Kinds of Discourses in Ordinary Conversation," "The Four Discourses," and "Vulgar Discourse," in *The Worlds Olio*, 15-19.

[69] The phrase *by reason* means "because" or "since."

As for the first, which is a discourse in the mind, which is reasoning, which reasoning is a discourse with things and not with words, as such a thing is not such a thing, and what such things are and what they are not, or in what such things agree or disagree, sympathy or antipathy, or such things resemble or not resemble, or on the cause of things or their effects or the like. This discourse is in the mind, which is distinguishing, and distinguishing belongs to judgment.

The second discoursing is with words, which is speech, and words are not things but only marks of things, or nicks or notches to know things by, and the tongue is the tally on which they are scored, for speech is a number of words, which words are made and joined together by the breath, tongue, teeth, and lips, and the continuance make a discourse, for a discourse is like a line or thread, whereon are a number of words strung, like as a chain of beads. If the words be well sorted and fitly and properly matched, as also evenly strung, the discourse is pleasant and delightful; this chain of discourse is longer or shorter, according as the speaker pleases. The third discourse is a discourse by signs, which is in actions; as some can discourse by the motion of their faces, countenances, hands, fingers, paces or measures, or by the cast of the eyes and many such, like postures, looks, actions, and several such ways of motion as have been invented to be understood. This and the first kind of discourse, as by things and motions, beasts may have, for ought we can know to the contrary. The last is by figures, or letters, prints, hieroglyphics, and painted stories, or engraven in metal or cut or carved in stone or molded or formed in earth, as clay or the like. In this kind of discourse, the pencil hath sometimes outdone the pen, as the painter hath outdone the historian and poet. This discoursing by signs or figures are discourses to the eye and not to the ear. There is also another kind or sort of discoursing which is hardly learned as yet because newly invented, or at lest, to what I have heard, which is by notes and several strains in the music.[70] I only mention it because I never heard it but once

---

[70] On the "application of certain aspects of the art of rhetoric to music" in the seventeenth century, see Gregory G. Butler, "Music and Rhetoric in Early Seventeenth-Century English Sources," *The Musical Quarterly* 66, no. 1 (1980): 53-64. Cavendish may also have encountered these ideas in France, where the composer and music theorist Bénigne de Bacilly argued that "singing airs is analogous to declaiming a discourse—'one must know how to sing well and declaim well at the same time'"; quoted in

and then I did not understand it, but yet it was by a skillful and ingenious musician which discoursed a story of his travels in his playing on a musical instrument, namely the harpsical.[71] But certainly, to my understanding or reason, it did seem a much easier way of discoursing than discoursing by actions or posture. But to end my discourse of discoursing, which discoursing may by several ways, several actions and postures, by several creatures, and in several languages, but reasoning is the soul's language, words the language of the senses, action the life's language, writing, printing, painting, carving, and molding are art's several languages, but music is the language of the gods.

Exeunt.

ACT 3, Scene 17

Enter two gentlemen.

FIRST GENTLEMAN. How do you like the ladies' discourse?

SECOND GENTLEMAN. As I like discourse.

FIRST GENTLEMAN. How is that?

SECOND GENTLEMAN. Why, I had rather hear a number of words than speak a number of words.

Catherine Gordon-Seifert, "Rhetoric and Expression in the Mid-Seventeenth-Century French Air: A Rationale for Compositional Style and Performance," Proceedings of the National Early Music Association International Conference, ed. Jon Potter and Johnathan Wainwright (University of York, 7-10 July 2009), https://www.york.ac.uk/music/conferences/nema/gordon-seifert/. For an extended analysis of the relationship between rhetoric and musical composition and performance, see her *Music and the Language of Love: Seventeenth-Century French Airs* (Bloomington: Indiana University Press, 2011). For such ideas applied to instrumental music, see Marot Martin, "The Rhetoric of *Mouvement* and Passionate Expression in Seventeenth-Century French Harpsichord Music," *Seventeenth Century French Studies* 31, no. 2 (2009): 137-49.

[71] A variant of the word "harpsichord," paralleling "virginal," an instrument in the harpsichord family.

FIRST GENTLEMAN. Then thou art not of the nature of mankind, for there is no man that had not rather speak than hear.

SECOND GENTLEMAN. No, it is a sign I am not of the nature of womankind that will hear nothing but will speak all; indeed, for the most part, they stop their ears with their tongues [or], at least, with the sound of their voices.

Exeunt.

ACT 3, Scene 18

Enter a company of gentlemen. The speaker takes the chair.

GENTLEMAN SPEAKER. It were too tedious to recite the several humors of the female sex, their scornful pride, their obstinate retired-ness,[72] their reserved coyness, their facile inconstancy, by which they become the most useless and most unprofitable creatures that nature hath made; but when they are joined to men, they are the most useful and most profitable creatures nature hath made. Wherefore, all those women that have common reason or sense of shame will never retire themselves from the company of men, for what women that have any consideration of honor, truth, or touch of goodness will be the worst of all creatures when they may be the best? But the truth of it is, women are spoiled by the over-fond dotage of men, for being flattered, they become so self-conceited as they think they were only made for the gods and not for men, and being mistresses of men's affections, they usurp their masculine power and authority and instead of being dutiful, humble, and obedient to men as they ought to be, they are tyrannical tyrannizers.

Exeunt.

---

[72] The word *retiredness* means, in the first sense, "withdrawn or reserved character, disposition, or behavior," but the word can also refer to a "way of life, characterized by privacy, quiet, or seclusion" (*OED*), certainly appropriate here, where the women are withdrawn into the Female Academy.

ACT 3, Scene 19

Enter two gentlemen.

FIRST GENTLEMAN. The young gallants,[73] methinks,[74] begin to be whetted[75] with anger.

SECOND GENTLEMAN. They have reason when the women have such dull, blunt appetites.[76]

Exeunt.

ACT 3, Scene 20

Enter the ladies of the academy. The lady speaker takes the chair.

MATRON. Ladies, let the theme of your discourse be, at this time, of friendship.[77]

LADY SPEAKER. This theme may more easily be discoursed of than friendship made,[78] by reason it is very difficult to make a right friendship, for hard it is to match men in agreeable humors, appetites, passions, capacities, conversations, customs, actions, natures, and dispositions, all which must be to make a true and lasting friendship; otherwise, two friends will be like two horses that draw contrary ways,[79] whereas souls, bodies, education, and lives must equally agree in friendship, for a worthy, honest man cannot be a friend to a base and unworthy man, by reason friendship is both an offensive and defensive league between two

---

[73] "A man of fashion and pleasure; a fine gentleman" (*OED*).

[74] "It seems to me," used parenthetically.

[75] Sharpened, especially referring to a weapon being sharpened in preparation for an attack.

[76] "Bent of the mind toward the attainment of an object or purpose; desire, inclination, disposition" (*OED*). The exchange between the gentlemen develops an interesting metaphor, since one of the most frequent figurative uses of the adjective *whetted* is to describe *appetite*.

[77] There are several reflections on friendship in *The Worlds Olio* (153-55).

[78] More simply, it is easier to talk of friendship than to develop a friendship.

[79] The comparison is to two horses yoked together that do not pull together.

souls and bodies, and no actions, either of the souls or bodies or any outward thing or fortune belonging thereunto, are to be denied. Wherefore knaves[80] with knaves and unworthy persons with unworthy persons may make a friendship, and honest men with honest men and worthy persons with worthy persons may do the like, but an honest man with a knave or a worthy person with a base[81] man or an honorable person with a mean[82] fellow, a noble soul with a base nature, a coward with a valiant man can make no true friendship. For, put the case[83] in such friendships my friend should desire me to do a base action for his sake, I must either break friendship or do unworthily, but as all worthy persons make Truth their goddess, which they seek and worship, honor the saint which they pray to, Virtue, the lady which they serve, so Honesty is the only friend they trust and rely on, and all the world is obliged to Honesty, for upright and just dealing.

Exeunt.

ACT 4, Scene 21

Enter two gentlemen.

FIRST GENTLEMAN. Methinks the women's lectural[84] discourse is better than the men's, for in my opinion, the men's discourses are simple, childish, and foolish in comparison of the women's.

SECOND GENTLEMAN. Why, the subject of the discourse is of women, which are simple, foolish, and childish.

---

[80] A *knave* may be a man of low social status, a peasant or a commoner, for example, but the word may also be used negatively, to refer to a "cunning unscrupulous rogue" or "villain" (*OED*).

[81] A person who belongs to the lower social classes, as opposed to a person *of worth*, that is "of note or standing" (*OED*).

[82] "Inferior in rank or quality," of "low social status," in particular a person "not of the nobility or gentry" (*OED*).

[83] The phrase is a technical one, meaning "to propound a hypothetical instance or illustration, to suppose; (in later use) to present a set of facts or arguments in support of a particular person, course of action, or version of events" (*OED*).

[84] "Of the nature of a lecture" (*OED*).

FIRST GENTLEMAN. There is no sign of their simplicity or folly in their discourse or speeches, I know not what may be in their actions.

SECOND GENTLEMAN. Now you come to the point, for the weakness of women lies in their actions, not in their words, for they have sharp wits and blunt judgments.

Exeunt.

ACT 4, Scene 22

Enter the ladies and grave matroness. The lady speaker takes the chair.

MATRONESS. Lady, let the theme of your discourse today be of a theater.

LADY SPEAKER. A theater is a public place for public actions, orations, disputations, presentations, whereunto is a public resort, but there are only two theaters which are the chief and the most frequented: the one is of war, the other of peace. The theater of war is the field, and the battles they fight are the plays they act, and the soldiers are the tragedians, and the theater of peace is the stage, and the plays there acted are the humors, manners, dispositions, natures, customs of men thereon described and acted, whereby the theaters are as schools to teach youth good principles and instruct them in the nature and customs of the world and mankind and learn[85] men to know themselves better than by any other way of instruction. And upon these theaters they may learn what is noble and good, what base and wicked, what is ridiculous and misbecoming, what graceful and best becoming, what to avoid and what to imitate. The genius that belongs to the theater of war is valor, and the genius that belongs to the theater of peace is wit; the designer of the rough plays of war is a general or council, the designer of the smooth plays of peace is a poet or a chief magistrate, but the difference of these plays acted on each theater is the one is real, the other feigned, the one in earnest, the other in jest, for a poet only feigns tragedies, but the soldiers do truly act tragedies. On the poetical theater I will only insist,

---

[85] While this use is considered nonstandard today, *learn* here means "teach" (and was an acceptable use, as the many contemporary examples cited in the *OED* illustrate).

for this theater belongs more to our persons and is a more fitter subject for the discourse of our sex than war is, for we delight more in scenes than in battles. I will begin first with poets who are the authors and makers of these kind of plays. Fame hath spoke loud, both of ancient and modern poets; as for the ancient poets, they are a length out of the reach of my judgment, so as my opinion will hardly reach so far, but as for our modern poets that have made plays in our modern times, although they deserve praise yet not so much nor so high applause as is given them, for most of their plots or foundation of their plays were taken out of old authors, as from the Greeks and Romans, historians and poets, also all the modern romances are taken out of these stories, and many plays out of these romances.[86]

MATRON. Lady, give me leave a little while to instruct you, as to tell you that all romances should be so, for the ground of a right romance is a true story; only falsehood is intermixed therein, so that a romance is a compound of truth and falsehood.

LADY SPEAKER. Give me leave to answer you that in my opinion a right romance is poetical fictions put into a historical style;[87] but for plays, the true comedy is pure love and humors, also the customs, manners, and the habits and inbred qualities of mankind, and right tragicomedies are the descriptions of the passions which are created in the soul, and a right tragedy is intermixed with the passions, appetites, and humors of men, with the influence of outward actions, accidents, and misfortunes. But as I said, some poets take the plots out of true history, others out of feigned history, which are romances, so as their plots (for the most part) are mere translations, and oft times the wit is also but a translated wit, only metamorphosed after their own way; but the truth is that some of them, their wit is their own and their plots were stolen or plainly taken,

---

[86] The lady speaker's criticism of contemporary playwrights in this speech and the next—that their work is derivative and thus should really be considered translation if not theft—is one that Cavendish the writer makes in her "General Prologue" (*Playes*, A7r-AA7r). On this see "Introduction," 60-61.

[87] Many of the young ladies' mandated themes for their discourses in the Female Academy are expansions of topics Cavendish addresses briefly in short paragraphs in *The Worlds Olio*, but here she actually quotes herself: "romance is as it were poetical fancies put into a historical style" ("What Romancy Is," *The Worlds Olio*, 9)

and some their plots are their own but the wit stolen, but of all theft, wit is never confessed, and some neither the plot nor wit is their own, and others both plots and wit are truly their own. These last poets (although but very few) are the true sons of Nature, the other but as adulterate issues. But for the most part, our modern plays, both plots and wit, are mere translations, and yet come out as boldly upon the stage as if the translators were the original authors, thinking, or at least hoping, that the alteration of the language conceals the theft, which to the unlearned it doth, but the learned soon find them out and see all their bodies, wings, legs, tail, and feathers, although they hide their head in the bush of ignorance. I speak not in discommendation of these translations nor translators, for translations are so far from being condemned as they ought to be much, nay very much, commended and highly praised, if it be such as is praiseworthy, for old authors may in some expressions be more profitable and good, both for wit and examples, than the modern, and the translators may be commended both for their judgment and learning; besides, very good translators must have a sympathetical genius with the original author. But their condemnation proceeds from the translators' unjust owning of it, upon themselves, or in translating it to the author's prejudice.

MATRON. Lady, let me interrupt you once again to ask your opinion how you like the Italian and French plays.

LADY SPEAKER. As well as I can like anything that is a strain beyond nature, or as I may say, nature's constraint, for the truth is, in their discourse or rehearsals, they do not only raise their voice a note or two too high, but many notes too high, and in their actions they are so forced as the spectators might very easily believe the actors would break their sinew strings,[88] and in their speech they fetch their breath so short and

---

[88] Sinews, or tendons, connect muscles with bones, and the lady speaker may have in mind a strain or similar kind of injury that could result from zealous over-acting; alternatively, animal tendons are used for bowstrings or in musical instruments, and the lady speaker may be imagining a bow pulled too taut or a stringed instrument plucked too forcefully.

thick and in such painful fetches[89] and throes[90] as those spectators that are strangers might verily believe that they were gasping for life.[91]

MATRON. But, lady, all know love, which is the theme or subject of plays, is a violent passion which forces the players to an elevation of action and speech.

LADY SPEAKER. Most reverend matron, my opinion is that though it be commendable and admirable for the poet to be elevated with a poetical divine inspiration to outdo nature, yet for the actors, their best grace is to play or act in the tracts or paths of nature and to keep within nature's bounds, and whensoever they go awry or transgress therefrom, they are to be condemned and to be accounted ill actors, and as for the passions of love, certainly the strongest love is like the deepest water, which is most silent and least unnecessarily active; they may sometimes murmur with winds of sighs, but never roar, they neither foam nor froth with violence, but are composed into a heavy body with a settled sadness. But in short, the Italian and French players act more romantical[92] than natural, which is feigned and constrained. But to conclude with the poet, he delights the ear and the understanding with the variety of everything that nature, hath made or art invented, for a poet is like a bee that gathers the sweet of every flower and brings the honey to his hive, which are the ears and memory of the hearers, or readers, in whose head his wit swarms; but as painters draw to the life, so poets should write to the life and players act to the life.

Exeunt.

---

[89] Deep breaths or sighs.

[90] Spasms, pangs, or convulsions.

[91] While the matron asks the lady speaker to assess French and Italian *plays*, the speaker comments instead on the actors, or *players*, and their style of acting, not on the plays themselves.

[92] Cavendish's use of *romantical* here is the first example cited in the *OED* for this variation of "romantic," meaning "overblown, euphuistic, flowery" (*OED*).

ACT 4, Scene [2]3[93]

Enter three gentlemen.

FIRST GENTLEMAN. The Academy of Ladies take no notice of the Academy of Men nor seem to consider what the men say, for they go on their own serious way and edifying discourses.

SECOND GENTLEMAN. At which the men are so angry as they have sworn to leave off talking and instead thereof they will sound trumpets so loud, when the ladies are in their discoursings, as they shall not hear themselves speak, by which means they hope to draw them out of their cloister as they swarm bees, for as bees gather together at the sound of a basin, kettle, or such like metaled thing, so they will disperse that swarm of academical ladies with the sound of brazen trumpets.

THIRD GENTLEMAN. Why, the ladies look through their grate upon the men whilst the men are speaking and seem to listen to what they speak, as the men do on and to the ladies.

SECOND GENTLEMAN. That is true, but they take no notice of them in their literal discourses, as what the men have said, for they neither mention the men nor their discoursing or arguments or academy, as if there were no such men.

Exeunt.

ACT 4, Scene 24

Enter the ladies and their matrons. The lady speaker takes the chair.

MATRON. Lady, let the theme of your discourse be, at this time, of vanity, vice, and wickedness.[94]

---

[93] The scene is incorrectly numbered as "Scene 13" in the original (*Playes*, 671).

[94] In the second part of *Natures Three Daughters*, Mademoiselle Grand Esprit (Wit) delivers a very similar, though somewhat shorter, "discourse" on vanity, vice, and wickedness to her audience (1.1).

LADY SPEAKER. There is a difference betwixt vanity, vice, and wickedness. Wickedness is in the will, vice in the desires, and vanity in the actions. Will proceeds from the soul, vice from the appetites, and action from custom or practice; the soul is produced from the gods, the appetites created by nature, and custom is derived from time. As for desires, we may desire and not will, and we may will and not act, and we may act and neither will nor desire, and we may desire, will, and act all at once, and to some particulars, we may neither desire, will, nor act; but the will makes vice wickedness, and vanity, vice. The willing of good proceeds from the gods, the willing of evil proceeds from the devils, so that sin is to will evil in despite of good, and piety is to will good in despite of evil, as neither the persuasions nor temptations of the one or the other shall draw our wills, for sin or wickedness is neither in the knowledge nor appetites. For if our great grandmother Eve had not willfully eat of that which was strictly forbidden her, she had not sinned, for if that she had only heard of the effects of that fruit or had desired it, yet had not willfully eaten thereof, she had never damned her posterity. Thus, to will against the gods' command is wickedness, but there is no such thing as wickedness in nature, but as I said wickedness proceeds from the soul, vice from the appetites, and vanity from the actions. As for wickedness, it is like a dead palsy,[95] it hath no sense or feeling of the grace or goodness of the gods, and vice is like an unwholesome meat, cut out by the appetites, for the appetites are like knives, whereas some are blunt, others are sharp and, as it were, too much edged, but they are either blunt or sharp according as nature whets them; but if they be very sharp as to be keen, they wound the body and make the life bleed. As for vanity, it is as the froth of life, it is light and swims atop, which bubbles out into extravagant and unprofitable actions, false opinions, and idle and impossible imaginations. But as I said, it is not the knowledge of vanity, vice, and wickedness that makes a creature guilty thereof, but the will and willful practice thereof, for wickedness, vice, and vanity must be known as much as piety, virtue, and discretion, otherwise men may run into evil through ignorance. Wherefore it is as great a shame to education not to be instructed in the bad as it is a glory to be instructed in the good. But the question will be

---

[95] A paralysis that affects all or part of the body, "producing complete insensibility or immobility of the part affected" (OED).

whether knowledge can be without a partaking thereof? I answer, not a perfect knowledge, but a suppositive[96] knowledge, for there are many things which cannot be perfectly known but suppositively known, so we must only know wickedness, vice, and vanity, as we do know the gods and devils, which is by a lively faith; so as we must be instructed in all that is pious, virtuous, and judicious as we are instructed of the power and goodness of the gods, and we must be instructed in all that is wicked, vicious, and idle as we are of the evil and power of the devils. Now I must inform you that there are three sorts of knowledge, as a knowledge of possession, a knowledge of action, and a knowledge of declaration. The knowledge of action lies in the appetites, the knowledge of declaration lies in the senses, the knowledge of possession in the will, action, and declarations. As for example, we may hear and see drunkenness, adultery, murder, theft, and the like, and have no appetite to the same actions; also we may have an appetite to the same actions, yet not a will to act the same; but if we have a desire and will act the same, we have, and are possessed with the most perfect knowledge thereof, but this last knowledge is utterly unlawful in things that are evil but not in things that are good. But to conclude, we must be instructed by a narrative way and by the intelligence of our ears and eyes in that which is evil as well, and as plainly, as in things that are good, not to be ignorant in anything that can be declared unto us, not staying until we be old, but to be thus instructed whilst we are young, for many that are young novices commit many evils through ignorance, not being instructed and informed plainly and clearly, but darkly and obscurely, caused by their foolish, cautionary, formal tutors or educators who hold that erroneous opinion that youth ought not to know such or such things or acts which, if they had known, evil might have been prevented and not left until their evil be known by practice, so that more evil is rather known by practice than declaration or instruction of information. But if our senses are a guide to our reason, and our reason a guide to our understanding, and that the reason and understanding governs our appetites, then 'is probable our sense, reason, and understanding may govern our will.

Exeunt.

---

[96] "Hypothetical, conjectural; supposed" (*OED*).

ACT 5, Scene 25

Enter the academical gentlemen.

FIRST GENTLEMAN. This is not to be suffered, for if we should let these ladies rest in peace and quiet in their enclosed habitation, we shall have none but old women, for all those young ladies that are not in the academy talk of nothing but of going into a female academy.

SECOND GENTLEMAN. You say true, insomuch as it begins to be a mode and a fashion for all the youngest, fairest, richest, and noblest ladies to enclose themselves into an academy.

THIRD GENTLEMAN. Nay, we must seek some way and devise some means to unroost them.

FOURTH GENTLEMAN. There is nothing can do it but noise, for they take such pleasure in the exercise of their tongues that unless we can put them to silence, there is no hopes to get them out.

F[IFTH] GENTLEMAN.[97] Trumpets, I doubt,[98] will not be loud enough.

SIXTH GENTLEMAN. Let us try.

ALL THE GENTLEMEN. Content,[99] content, etc.[100]

Exeunt.

---

[97] Although this speech is attributed to "*1. Gent.*" in *Playes*, it falls between speeches of the fourth and sixth gentlemen, and so it has been emended to "Fifth Gentleman" here.

[98] I fear.

[99] *Content* here is used as an exclamation of agreement or assent ("I am content," "Agreed!").

[100] By her use of *etc.* (spelled "&c" in *Playes*), Cavendish suggests the gentlemen's exclamations continue as they exit.

ACT 5, Scene 26

Enter the ladies and the grave matrons. The lady speaker takes the chair.

MATRON. Lady, let the theme of your discourse be at this time of boldness and bashfulness.[101]

LADY SPEAKER. There are three sorts of boldness or confidence; the one proceeds from custom or practice, as it may be observed by preachers, pleaders, and players, that can present themselves, speak and act freely in a public assembly.

The second sort of boldness or confidence proceeds from ignorance, not foreseeing what errors or follies may be committed or chance to fall out or what is fittest to be done or said, like as poor, mean, country people, who have neither birth nor breeding, have so much confidence as they can more confidently present themselves or presence to those of noble birth and breeding and can more freely and boldly talk to any person or persons of what quality or dignity soever than those noble persons can talk to them.

The third and last sort of confidence or boldness proceeds from an extraordinary opinionatedness[102] or self-conceitedness, for those that think or believe themselves to be above others in wit, person, parts, or power, although they have neither, will be most haughtily and proudly confident, scorning and undervaluing all others as inferior. Thus bold confidence, or confident boldness, is produced from practice, ignorance, and pride.

Also there are three sorts of bashfulness.

The one proceeds from too great an apprehension.[103]

---

[101] Cavendish writes at some length on the topic "Of Boldness and Bashfulness" in *The Worlds Olio*, 88-89.

[102] Cavendish's use of *opinionatedness* (the "quality of being opinionated") here in *The Female Academy* is the earliest use of the word cited in the *OED*.

[103] "The action of 'feeling' anything emotionally; sensitiveness or sensibility to; sympathetic perception" (*OED*).

The other from a poetical fiction.

The third from an aspiring ambition.

First, from too great an apprehension, as some are afraid that their observers or friends should make an evil construction of their good intentions. Others will be bashful and out of countenance[104] upon a poetical fiction, as imagining of some impossible or at least some improbable accident which may fall out to their disgrace. The third and last is through an aspiring ambition, desiring to out-act all others in excellencies and, fearing to fail therein, is apt to be out of countenance as if they had received a foil.[105] Thus we may perceive that the stream of good nature, the piercing beams of wit, and the throne of noble ambition is the true cause of bashfulness, I mean not shamefastness,[106] but sweet bashfulness. But although bashfulness is a sweet, tender, noble, and piercing effect of and from the soul, yet bashfulness is apt to unstring the nerves, to weaken the sinews, to dull the senses, to quench the spirits, to blunt the eyes or points of wit, and to obstruct the speech, insomuch as to cause the words to run stumblingly out of the mouth or to suffer none to pass forth, but a little anger in the mind will take off the extreme bashfulness of the behavior, although much anger doth obstruct the senses, spirits, and speech as much as extreme bashfulness doth, for extreme anger and extreme bashfulness have often one and the same effects to outward appearance.

Exeunt.

---

[104] The phrase *out of countenance* means to be "disconcerted, abashed" (*OED*).

[105] To *receive a foil* is to experience a "repulse, defeat in an onset or enterprise; a baffling check" (*OED*).

[106] Cavendish distinguishes carefully between *shamefastness*, a feeling of shame, and true *bashfulness*. Since Cavendish herself was a woman who was frequently described as extremely bashful, we might conclude that this third cause of bashfulness, "aspiring" and "noble" ambition, is the source of her suffering—the dire consequences of such bashfulness are described by the lady speaker.

ACT 5, Scene 27

Enter two gentlemen.

FIRST GENTLEMAN. The gentlemen will turn trumpeters, for a regiment of gentlemen have bought every one of them a trumpet to sound a march to the academy of ladies.

[SECOND] GENTLEMAN.[107] Faith, if the ladies would answer their trumpets with blowing of horns,[108] they would serve them but as they ought to be served.

FIRST GENTLEMAN. Women will sooner make horns than blow horns.[109]

Exeunt

ACT 5, Scene 28

Enter the lady and their matroness. The lady speaker takes the chair.

MATRON. Lady, let the theme of your discourse at this time be of virtuous courtships and wooing suitors.

---

[107] Although this speech is attributed to "*1. Gent.*" in *Playes*, with three successive speeches thus attributed to the same character, the two gentlemen who enter the scene are clearly intended to be having a conversation.

[108] The second gentleman seems to suggest that the ladies might fight back against the trumpeting gentlemen by drowning out the din with their own instruments (*horns*), but he may also be suggesting something less ladylike—*to make horns at* someone, making a fist while extending two fingers, is to offer an insulting or derisive gesture (*OED*).

[109] The first gentleman's response, continuing the punning on *horn*, can be read in a couple of ways. First, *horn* may refer to an erect penis—thus he may be saying that the ladies will cause the gentlemen to become sexually excited. But since a cuckold (a husband of an unfaithful wife) was also said to have horns, the gentleman may, alternatively, be suggesting that the ladies are more likely to betray men than simply to blow an instrument and make noise.

LADY SPEAKER. Some poetical and romantical writers make valiant, gallant heroics[110] woo poorly, sneakingly, and peddlingly.[111]

MATRON. Lady, let me interrupt you. Would you have gallant heroics in their courtships to fair young ladies as commanding as in the field or as furious as in a battle?

LADY SPEAKER. No, I would have them woo with a confident behavior, a noble demeanor, a generous civility, and not to be amazed or to tremble for fear, to weep for pity, to kneel for mercy, to sigh and be dejected with a mistress's frown, for though sorrow, sighs, tears, and humility become all heroic spirits very well and express a noble and generous soul, yet not in such a cause, for tears become all heroic spirits for the death or torments of friends or for the sufferances of innocents or virtue, yet not if only themselves were tormented or to die or for any misfortune that could come upon our own persons or estates or for any obstructions to their own pleasures or delights, but it becomes all heroic spirits to tremble for fear of their honor or loss of their fame and expresses a generous soul to grieve and to mourn in a general calamity and to humble themselves to the gods for those in distress and to implore and kneel to them for mercy, both for themselves and others, as for to divert the wrath of the gods, but not to weep, sigh, tremble, kneel, pray for their effeminate pleasures, delights, or societies, nor to grieve or sorrow for the loss of the same.

Also, some writers, when they are to describe a bashful and modest lady, such as are nobly and honorably bred, describe them as if they were simply shamefaced, which description makes such appear as if they came merely from the milk bowl and had been bred only with silly housewives, and that their practice was to pick worms from roots of flowers and their pastimes to carry and fling crumbs of bread to birds or little chickens that were hatched by their hens their mothers gave them or to gather a lapful of sweet flowers to distill a little sweet water to dip their

[110] The word *heroic* can be used as a noun meaning "a hero"; the word can also refer to a member of the Royalist party during the English civil wars (*OED*).
[111] In a contemptible, trifling, or ineffectual manner.

handkerchiefs in or to wash their faces in a little rosewater;[112] and indeed, this harmless and innocent breeding may be modest and bashful or, rather, shamefaced for want of other conversation, which custom and company will soon cast off or wear out and then print boldness on their brow, but true, modest souls, which have for the most part bashful countenances, proceed from a deep apprehension, a clear understanding, an ingenuous wit, a thinking brain, a pure mind, a refined spirit, a noble education, and not from an ignorant, obscure breeding; for it is not ignorance that makes modesty, but knowledge, nor is it guiltiness that makes bashfulness, but fear of those that are guilty. But as I said, many writers that would make a description of modest and bashful women mistake and express a shamefaced ignorance and obscure breeding, and instead of expressing a young lady to be innocent of faults, they express her to be one that is ignorant of knowledge, so as when they would describe a modest, bashful, innocent virgin, they mistake and describe a simple, ignorant, shamefaced maid that either wants breeding or capacity.

MATRON. But, lady, let me ask you one question. Would you have a young virgin as confident and knowing as a married wife?

LADY SPEAKER. Yes, although not in their behavior or condition of life, but in her virtue and constancy, for a chaste married wife is as modest and bashful as a virgin, though not so simple, ignorant, and shamefaced as a plain-bred maid. But as I said, writers should describe the wooing of gallant heroics or great and noble persons to woo with a generous confidence or manly garb, a civil demeanor, a rational discourse, to an honest design and to a virtuous end, and not with a whining voice, in pitiful words and fawning language, and if it be only for a mistress, as for a courtesan, bribes are the best advocates or to employ others to treat with them and not to be the pimp, although for themselves.

---

[112] All of the details in this passage suggest that unsuccessful writers who incorrectly describe "modest" and "bashful" ladies (which Cavendish has "correctly" defined, above, 5.26) make them sound as if they are women of classes less elevated than that of the well-born young women in the Female Academy—simple and ignorant or inexperienced country women rather than the truly "modest" and "bashful" ladies.

Also, writers should when they describe noble virgins to receive noble addresses of love and to receive those noble addresses or courtships with an attentive modesty in a bashful countenance, and if to tremble for fear, to describe the fear as being the nature of the sex; also to describe their behavior after a noble garb[113] and their answers to their suitors to be full of reason, sense, and truth, and those answers to be delivered in as short discourses and as few words as civility will allow of and not like an ignorant innocent, a childish simplicity, an unbred behavior, expressing themselves or answering their suitors with mincing words that have neither sense nor reason in them.

Also, poetical and romantical writers should not make great princes that have been bred in great and populous cities, glorious camps, and splendorous courts to woo and make love like private-bred[114] men or like rude-bred clowns[115] or like mean-bred[116] servants or like scholars that woo by the book in scholastical[117] terms or phrases or to woo like flaunting, ranting, swearing, bragging swaggerers or roosters[118] or to woo a country wench like as a noble lady or great princess.

Also, not to make such women as have been bred and born nobly and honorably to receive the courtship of great persons like a dairymaid, kitchen maid, or like such as have been bred in mean cottages as to behave themselves simply or rudely as to the answer and speak crossingly or thwartingly as contradicting every word that is spoken unto them, as if they did believe what they said was not truth, for civil and honorably bred women who have noble and generous souls will rather seem to believe all their superlative praises than make doubts, as if they knew they lied, for to make doubts is in the mid-way to give the lie.[119]

---

[113] Used here, *garb* refers to a "person's outward bearing, behavior, carriage, or demeanour" (*OED*).

[114] Probably meaning "deprived" or "dispossessed."

[115] A *clown* is a peasant or rustic, the word also implying someone who is ignorant and uncouth.

[116] To be *meanly bred* is to be someone of low social status—as, here, a servant.

[117] Academic in a negative sense—"pedantic, unduly formal or subtle" (*OED*).

[118] In addition to its common meaning of a male domestic fowl, a *rooster* is a "violent or disorderly person" or a "boastful" person, thus a perfect companion for a *swaggerer*.

[119] To *give the lie* is to accuse someone to his or her face of being a liar.

MATRON. Lady, how approve you of those lovers that kiss the letters, tokens, pledges, and the like that are sent unto them from their lovers, or such as wear letters, tokens, or pledges in their bosoms and next their hearts and take them and view them a hundred times a day?

LADY SPEAKER. Approve it, say you? You mean disapprove it. But let me tell you, most reverend matron, that the very hearing of it makes me sick, and the seeing of it would make me die.

I have so great an aversion against such actions, for those actions, like as whining speeches, proceed from filthy, amorous[120] love and mean lovers, for true love in noble persons receives gifts as an expression of their suitors' or lovers' loves and will carefully keep them as an acknowledgment of the receipt and accept of them as a great seal to their affections, yet they keep such presents but as treasurers, not as owners, until they be man and wife. Neither do they make idols of such gifts, nor do they adore the owner the more for the gift nor the gift for the owner, nor do they think fit they ought to give such outward expressions of love by such useless actions whenas they have a high esteem of their suitor's love, a perfect belief of their merit and a constant return of their affection, and a resolution to die or suffer any misery for their sakes if need required. Besides, true lovers have ever the idea of their beloved in their thoughts, by which they cannot forget their memory; indeed, love letters they may read often because letters are an enjoyment of their discourse, although their persons be at a distance, and are also a recreation and delight in their wits, if there be any wit therein,[121] but to kiss the paper, they neither find pleasure, delight, nor profit, neither to

---

[120] As it is used by the lady speaker here, and below, *amorous* is clearly negative (love that is amorous is *filthy*), referring to a kind of sexual desire rather than true love, as the lady speaker (and Cavendish herself, perhaps) defines it.

[121] During their courtship, William Cavendish and the young Margaret Lucas exchanged letters, some of them, from William, quite passionate (in one of her letters to him she responds to the bawdy "love" poems he has sent her); see *The Phanseys of William Cavendish Marquis of Newcastle Addressed to Margaret Lucas and Her Letters in Reply*, ed. Douglas Grant (London: The Nonesuch Press, 1956). For a more recent edition of the correspondence, see Anna Battigelli, *Margaret Cavendish and the Exiles of the Mind* (Lexington: The University Press of Kentucky, 1998), Appendix B: "The Letters of Margaret Lucas Addressed to William Cavendish" (119-32). On this exchange of letters, see also James Fitzmaurice, "The Intellectual and Literary Courtship of Margaret Cavendish," *Early Modern Literary Studies* Special Issue 14 (May 2004): 7.1-16.

themselves nor to their beloved. The truth is, not one writer amongst a thousand make lovers woo either wisely, wittily, nobly, eloquently, or naturally, but either foolishly, meanly, unmanly, unhandsomely, or amorously, which is corruptly.

MATRON. Lady, you say very true, and some romantical writers make long and tedious orations or long and tedious and fruitless discourse in such times as requires sudden action.

LADY SPEAKER. You say right, as to speak when they are to fight, but for my part, I hate to read romances or some scenes in plays whose ground or foundation is amorous love.

MATRON. When you read such books, you must never consider the subject that the writer writes on, but consider the wit, language, fancy, or description.

SECOND MATRON. Most reverend sister, I suppose few read romances or the like books but for the wit, fancy, judgment, and lively descriptions, for they do not read such books as they do read chronicles, wherein is only to be considered the true relation of the history.

LADY SPEAKER. Most grave and wise matroness, I believe though none read romances or such like books whose ground is feigned love and lovers as they read chronicles whose ground should be unfeigned truth, yet certainly few read romances or the like books either for the wit, fancy, judgment, or descriptions, but to feed their amorous humors on their amorous discourses and to tune their voice to their amorous strains of amorous love, for it is to be observed that those books that are most amorously penned are most often read.

Exeunt.

Scene the last [ACT 5, Scene 29]

Enter the academical gentlemen. To them enters a servant.

MANSERVANT. May it please your worships,[122] there is an ancient gentlewoman that desires to speak with your worships.

FIRST GENTLEMAN. I lay my life it is one of the matrons of the academy.

SECOND GENTLEMAN. Faith, if the humble-bee[123] is flown out, the rest of the bees will follow.

THIRD GENTLEMAN. I fear if they do—they will swarm about our ears.

FOURTH GENTLEMAN. Yes, and sting us with their tongues.

FIFTH GENTLEMAN. Let us send for her in.

SIXTH GENTLEMAN. I will go and usher her in.

He goes out [then] enters with the matron. All the gentlemen pull off their hats.

MATRON. Gentlemen, the ladies of the academy have sent me unto you to know the reason or cause that you will not let them rest in quiet or suffer them to live in peace, but disturb them in both by a confused noise of trumpets, which you uncivilly and discourteously blow at their grate and gates.

FIRST GENTLEMAN. The cause is that they will not permit us to come into their company but have barricadoed[124] their gates against us and

---

[122] This is a title of honor; in this case, the manservant uses it when he speaks to the gentlemen, who are of a higher social status.

[123] A *humble-bee* is a large bee "which makes a loud humming sound," according to the *OED*. The second gentleman seems to believe that if the large bee emerges from the hive, the smaller bees will follow.

[124] A wonderful verb, *to barricado* (from the French *barricade* or the Spanish *barricada*, casks used to create hastily constructed street barriers) means to "enclose (a person) with a barricade; to shut up, bar in securely" or to "fortify or defend (a place) with or

have encloistered themselves from us; besides, it is a dangerous example for all the rest of their sex, for if all women should take a toy[125] in their heads to encloister themselves, there would be none left out to breed on.

MATRON. Surely it is very fit and proper that young virgins should live a retired life, both for their education and reputation.

SECOND GENTLEMAN. As for their education, it is but to learn to talk, and women can do that without teaching, for on my conscience, a woman was the first inventor of speech,[126] and as for their retirement, nature did never make them for that purpose, but to associate themselves with men. And since men are the chief head of their kind, it were a sign they had but very little brain if they would suffer the youngest and fairest women to encloister themselves.

MATRON. Gentlemen, pray give me leave to inform you, for I perceive you are in great error of mistake, for these ladies have not vowed virginity [n]or are they encloistered, for an academy is not a cloister but a school wherein are taught how to be good wives when they are married.

THIRD GENTLEMAN. But no man can come to woo them to be wives.

MATRON. No, but if they can win their parents or those they are left in trust with and get their good liking and consent, the young ladies have learned so much duty and obedience as to obey to what they shall think fit.

FOURTH GENTLEMAN. But we desire the ladies' good liking. We care not for their friends, for the approvement and good liking of their friends, without the love of the ladies, will not make us happy, for there

---

as with barricades"—both appropriate here, where the young ladies are enclosed within the Female Academy.

[125] Take a foolish fancy or act on a whim.

[126] The second gentleman is clearly enjoying a sexist joke here, but perhaps he is also referring to the Greek goddess Mnemosyne, the daughter of Cronus and Gaia; the goddess of memory and the mother of the Muses, Mnemosyne was also credited with naming things, thus creating words and language.

is no satisfaction in a secondary love, as to be beloved for another's sake and not for their own.

MATRON. If you be worthy gentlemen, as I believe you all are, their love will be due to your merits, and your merits will persuade them to love you.

ALL THE GENTLEMEN. Well, if you will be our mediator, we will surcease our clamor; otherwise we will increase our noise.

MATRON. If you can get leave of their parents and friends, I will endeavor to serve you and shall be proud of the employment that you shall be pleased to impose to my trust and management.

GENTLEMEN. And we shall be your servants, for your favors.

They all go out, with the gentlemen waiting on her, with their hats in their hands, scraping[127] *and congying*[128] *to her.*

FINIS

_____

[127] "To make obeisance, to bow drawing the foot back" (*OED*).

[128] The phrase used here, *scraping and congying*, seems to be use in place of the more frequently used phrase "bowing and scraping," a "contemptuous reference to over-ceremonious politeness or reference" (*OED*). The word *congy* itself refers to taking leave or departing, so the stage direction may also simply mean that the gentlemen bow and bid the matron farewell.

Select Bibliography

Primary Sources

Original Collections of Plays Published by Margaret Cavendish

Cavendish, Margaret. *Playes*. London, 1662.

————. *Plays, Never before Printed*. London, 1668.

Additional Primary Sources

Cavendish, Margaret. *The Life of the thrice Noble, High and Puissant Prince William Cavendishe, Duke, Marquess, and Earl of Newcastle. . . .* London, 1667. In *The Life of William Cavendish, Duke of Newcastle, . . . by Margaret, Duchess of Newcastle*. Edited by Charles H. Firth, 1-147. 2nd rev. ed. New York: E. P. Dutton, 1907.

————. *A True Relation of my Birth, Breeding and Life*. London, 1656. In Firth, ed., *The Life of William Cavendish*, 155-78.

Cavendish, William, ed. *Letters and Poems in Honour of the Incomparable Princess, Margaret, Dutchess of Newcastle*. London, 1676.

Cerasano, S. P., and Marion Wynne-Davies, eds. *Renaissance Drama by Women: Texts and Documents*. New York: Routledge, 1996.

Conway, Anne Finch. *The Conway Letters: The Correspondence of Anne, Viscountess Conway, Henry More, and Their Friends, 1642-1684*. Edited by Marjorie Hope Nicholson and Sarah Hutton. Rev. ed. New York: Oxford University Press, 1992

Evelyn, John. *The Diary of John Evelyn.* Vol. 2. Edited by William Bray. London: George Bell, 1889.

Evelyn, Mary. "Letters of Mrs. Evelyn." In *The Diary and Correspondence of John Evelyn.* Vol. 4. Edited by William Bray, 3-43. London: Henry Colburn, 1857.

Huygens, Constijn. *Die Briefwisseling van Constantijn Huygens, 1608-1687.* 6 vols. Edited by J. A. Worp. The Hague: Martinus Nijhoff, 1911-16. Reprinted Huygens ING, 2010, http://resources.huygens.knaw.nl/briefwisseling-constantijnhuygens.

Osborne, Dorothy. *The Letters of Dorothy Osborne to Sir William Temple.* Edited by Edward A. Parry. New York: E. P. Dutton, 1914,

Pepys, Samuel. *The Diary of Samuel Pepys* . . . . 8 vols. Edited by Henry B. Wheatley. New York: Macmillan, 1892-96.

Prynne, William. *Histrio-mastix: The Players Scourge, or, Actors Tragedie, Divided into Two Parts.* . . . London, 1633.

Thompson, Edward M. *Correspondence of the Family of Hatton . . . 1607-1704.* Camden Society n. s., vol. 22. London: Camden Society, 1878.

Select Secondary Sources

Complete bibliographical information for all sources consulted in this edition is provided in the notes. Included here are biographies of Margaret Cavendish, works that focus on women and drama in early-modern England, and critical studies of Margaret Cavendish's plays, in particular of *The Female Academy*.

Andrea, Bernadette. "Coming Out in Margaret Cavendish's Closet Dramas." *In-between* 9 (2000): 219-41.

Baker-Putt, Alyce R. "Redefining the Female Self through Female Communities: Margaret Cavendish's *The Female Academy, The Convent of Pleasure,* and *Bell in Campo.*" *Shakespeare and Renaissance Association of West Virginia* 29 (2006): 37-46.

Bennett, Alexandra G. "Fantastic Realism: Margaret Cavendish and the Possibilities of Drama." In Cottegnies and Weitz, *Authorial Conquests*, 179-94.

———. "Happy Families and Learned Ladies: Margaret Cavendish, William Cavendish, and Their Onstage Academy Debate." *Early Modern Literary Studies: A Journal of Sixteenth- and Seventeenth-Century English Literature* Special Issue 14 (2004): 3.1-14. http://extra.shu.ac.uk/emls/si-14/bennhapp.html.

Billing, Valerie. "'Treble marriage': Margaret Cavendish, William Newcastle, and Collaborative Authorship Author(s)." *Journal for Early Modern Cultural Studies* 11, no. 2 (2011): 94-122.

Bonin, Erin Lang. "Margaret Cavendish's Dramatic Utopias and the Politics of Gender." *Studies in English Literature, 1500-1900* 40, no. 2 (2000): 339-54.

Britland, Karen. *Drama at the Courts of Henrietta Maria*. New York: Cambridge University Press, 2006.

Brown, Pamela, and Peter Parolin, eds. *Women Players in England, 1500–1650: Beyond the All-Male Stage*. Studies in Performance and Early Modern Drama. Burlington, VT: Ashgate Publishing, 2005.

Bullard, Rebecca. "Gatherings in Exile: Interpreting the Bibliographical Structure of *Natures Pictures Drawn by Fancies Pencil to the Life* (1656)." *English Studies* 92, no. 7 (2011): 786-805.

Cerasano, S. P., and Marion Wynne-Davies, eds. *Readings in Renaissance Women's Drama: Criticism, History, and Performance, 1594-1998*. New York: Routledge, 1998.

Chalmers, Hero. "'The Gallery of Heroick Women': Margaret Cavendish and the Images of the Author." In *Royalist Women Writers, 1650-1680*, 16–55. Oxford English Monographs. New York: Oxford University Press, 2004.

————. "The Politics of Feminine Retreat in Margaret Cavendish's *The Female Academy* and *The Convent of Pleasure*." *Women's Writing* 6, no. 1 (1999): 81-94.

Cottegnies, Line, and Nancy Weitz, eds. *Authorial Conquests: Essays on Genre in the Writing of Margaret Cavendish*. Madison, NJ: Fairleigh Dickinson University Press, 2003.

Cotton, Nancy. *Women Playwrights in England, c. 1363-1750*. Lewisburg, PA: Bucknell University Press, 1980.

Cuder-Dominguez, Pilar. "Re-Crafting the Heroic, Constructing a Female Hero: Margaret Cavendish and Aphra Behn." *SEDERI: Yearbook of the Spanish and Portuguese Society for English Renaissance* 17 (2007): 27-45.

————. *Stuart Women Playwrights, 1613-1713*. Studies in Performance and Early Modern Drama. Burlington, VT: Ashgate Publishing, 2010.

Findlay, Alison. *Playing Spaces in Early Women's Drama*. New York: Cambridge University Press, 2006.

Findlay, Alison, Gweno Williams, and Stephanie J. Hodgson-Wright. "'The play is ready to be acted': Women and Dramatic Production, 1570-1670." *Women's Writing* 6, no. 1 (1999): 129-48.

Findlay, Alison, Stephanie Hodgson-Wright, and Gweno Williams, eds. *Women and Dramatic Production, 1550-1700*. Longman Medieval and Renaissance Library. New York: Routledge, 2000.

Finke, Laurie A. *Women's Writing in English: Medieval England*. Women's Writing in English. New York: Longman, 1999.

Fitzmaurice, James. "Cavendish, Margaret, duchess of Newcastle upon Tyne (1623?-1673)." *Oxford Dictionary of National Biography* [online]. Oxford: Oxford University Press, 2004-. Article published 2004. http://oxforddnb.com.

———. "Fancy and the Family: Self-Characterizations of Margaret Cavendish." *HLQ* 53 (1990): 198-209.

———. "Margaret Cavendish on Her Own Writing: Evidence from Revision and Handmade Correction." *Papers of the Bibliographical Society of America* 85, no. 3 (1991): 297-307.

Grant, Douglas. *Margaret the First: A Biography of Margaret Cavendish, Duchess of Newcastle, 1623-1673.* London: Rupert Hart-Davis, 1957.

Greenstadt, Amy. "Margaret's Beard." *Early Modern Women: An Interdisciplinary Journal* 5 (2010): 171-82.

Hiscock, Andrew. "'Here's No Design, No Plot, nor Any Ground': The Drama of Margaret Cavendish and the Disorderly Woman." *Women's Writing* 4, no. 3 (1997): 401-20.

Howe, Elizabeth. *The First English Actresses: Women and Drama, 1660-1700.* New York: Cambridge University Press, 1992.

Jagodzinski. Cecile M. *Privacy and Print: Reading and Writing in Seventeenth-Century England.* Charlottesville: University Press of Virginia, 1999.

Jankowski, Theodora A. "Critiquing the Sexual Economies of Marriage." In *The History of British Women's Writing,* vol. 3. *1610-1690.* Edited by Mihoko Suzuki, 221-37. New York: Palgrave Macmillan, 2011.

Jansen, Sharon L. *Reading Women's Worlds from Christine de Pizan to Doris Lessing: A Guide to Six Centuries of Women Writers Imagining Rooms of Their Own.* New York: Palgrave Macmillan, 2011.

Jones, Kathleen. *A Glorious Fame: The Life of Margaret Cavendish, Duchess of Newcastle, 1623-1673.* London: Bloomsbury Publishing, 1988.

Kelly, Erna. "Playing with Religion: Convents, Cloisters, Martyrdom, and Vows." *Early Modern Literary Studies: A Journal of Sixteenth- and Seventeenth-Century English Literature* Special Issue 14 (2004): 4.1-24. http://extra.shu.ac.uk/emls/si-14/kellplay.html.

Kramer, Annette. "'Thus by the musick of a ladyes tongue': Margaret Cavendish's Dramatic Innovations in Women's Education." *Women's History Review* 2, no. 1 (1993): 57-79.

Leduc, Guyonne. "Women's Education in Margaret Cavendish's Plays." *Cercles* 4 (2002): 16-38.

Masten, Jeffrey. "Material Cavendish: Paper, Performance, 'Sociable Virginity.'" *Modern Language Quarterly* 65 (2004): 49–68.

————. *Textual Intercourse: Collaboration, Authorship, and Sexualities in Renaissance Drama.* Cambridge Studies in Renaissance Literature and Culture. New York: Cambridge University Press, 1997.

McManus, Clare. *Women on the Renaissance Stage: Anna of Denmark and Female Masquing in the Stuart Court, 1590-1619.* Manchester, UK: Manchester University Press, 2002.

Mendelson, Sara. "Playing Games with Gender and Genre: The Dramatic Self-Fashioning of Margaret Cavendish." In Cottegnies and Weitz, *Authorial Conquests*, 195-212.

Mosher, Joyce Devlin. "Female Spectacle as Liberation in Margaret Cavendish's Plays." *Early Modern Literary Studies: A Journal of Sixteenth- and Seventeenth-Century English Literature* 11, no. 1 (2005): 7.1-28. http://extra.shu.ac.uk/emls/11-1/moshcave.htm.

Normington, Katie. *Gender and Medieval Drama.* Gender in the Middle Ages. Cambridge, UK: D. S. Brewer, 2004.

Orgel, Stephen. *Impersonations: The Performance of Gender in Shakespeare's England.* New York: Cambridge University Press, 1996.

Payne, Linda R. "Dramatic Dreamscape: Women's Dreams and Utopian Vision in the Works of Margaret Cavendish, Duchess of Newcastle." In *Curtain Calls: British and American Women and the Theater, 1660-1820.* Edited by Mary Anne Schofield and Cecilia Macheski, 18-33. Athens: Ohio University Press, 1991.

Pearson, Jacqueline. "'Women May Discourse . . . as Well as Men': Speaking and Silent Women in the Plays of Margaret Cavendish, Duchess of Newcastle." *Tulsa Studies in Women's Literature* 4, no. 1 (1985): 33-45.

Poole, William. "Margaret Cavendish's Books in New College, and around Oxford." *New College Notes* 6 (2015): 1-8. http://www.new.ox.ac.uk/ncnotes.

Raber, Karen. *Dramatic Difference: Gender, Class, and Genre in the Early Modern Closet Drama.* Newark: University of Delaware Press, 2001.

———. "'Our Wits Joined as in Matrimony': Margaret Cavendish's *Playes* and the Drama of Authority." *English Literary Renaissance* 28, no. 3 (1998): 464-93.

Romack, Katherine, and James Fitzmaurice, eds. *Cavendish and Shakespeare, Interconnections.* Burlington, VT: Ashgate Publishing, 2006.

Schabert, Ina. "The Theatre in the Head: Performances of the Self, by the Self, for the Self." In *Solo Performances: Staging the Early Modern Self in England.* Edited by Ute Berns, 33-48. Internationale Forschungen Zur Allgemeinen Und Vergleichende. New York: Editions Rodopi, 2010.

Shaver, Anne. "Agency and Marriage in the Fictions of Lady Mary Wroth and Margaret Cavendish, Duchess of Newcastle." In *Pilgrimage for Love: Essays in Early Modern Literature in Honor of Josephine A. Roberts,* 177-90. Edited by Sigrid King and Josephine A. Roberts. Medieval & Renaissance Texts & Studies. Tempe: Arizona Center for Medieval and Renaissance Studies, 1999.

Straznicky, Marta. *Privacy, Playreading, and Women's Closet Drama, 1550–1700.* New York: Cambridge University Press, 2004.

———. "Reading the Stage: Margaret Cavendish and Commonwealth Closet Drama." *Criticism* 37, no. 3 (1995): 355-90.

Tomlinson, Sophie. *Women on Stage in Stuart Drama.* New York: Cambridge University Press, 2005.

Venet, Gisele. "Margaret Cavendish's Dramas: An Aesthetic of Fragmentation." In Cottegnies and Weitz, *Authorial Conquests*, 213-28.

Whitaker, Katie. *Mad Madge: The Extraordinary life of Margaret Cavendish, Duchess of Newcastle, the First Woman to Live by her Pen*. New York: Basic Books, 2002.

Wiseman, Susan. *Drama and Politics in the English Civil War*. New York, Cambridge University Press, 1998.

Wood, Tanya. "Margaret Cavendish, Duchess of Newcastle, *The Convent of Pleasure* (1668), Ending Revised by Her Husband, the Duke of Newcastle." In *Reading Early Modern Women: An Anthology of Texts in Manuscript and Print, 1550-1700*. Edited by Helen Ostovich and Elizabeth Sauer, 435-37. New York: Routledge, 2004.

Woolf, Virginia. *The Common Reader, First Series*. 1925. Reprint, New York: Houghton Mifflin / Mariner Books, 2002.

———. *A Room of One's Own*. 1929. Reprint, New York: Harcourt / Harvest Edition, 1989.

Wynne-Davies, Marion. "The Theater." In *The History of British Women's Writing*, vol. 2, *1500-1610*. Edited by Caroline Bicks and Jennifer Summit, 175-95. New York: Palgrave Macmillan, 2010.

Suggestions for Further Reading

Listed here are a few key resources for readers who may be interested in further discussion of Cavendish's philosophical, theological, scientific, and political work, as well as her writing in other genres, including prose, poetry, biography, autobiographical narrative, and letters.

Battigelli, Anna. *Margaret Cavendish and the Exiles of the Mind*. Studies in the English Renaissance. Lexington: University of Kentucky Press, 1998.

Broad, Jacqueline. "Margaret Cavendish." In *Women Philosophers of the Seventeenth Century*, 35–64. New York: Cambridge University Press, 2003.

Broad, Jacqueline, and Karen Green. "Margaret Cavendish, Duchess of Newcastle." In *A History of Women's Political Thought in Europe, 1400–1700*, 199–224. New York: Cambridge University Press, 2009.

Clucas, Stephen, ed. *A Princely Brave Woman: Essays on Margaret Cavendish, Duchess of Newcastle*. Burlington, VT: Ashgate Publishing, 2003.

Cunning, David. "Margaret Lucas Cavendish." In *The Stanford Encyclopedia of Philosophy* [online]. Stanford University, 1997-. Winter 2016 Edition. http://plato.stanford.edu/entries/margaret-cavendish/.

Dodds, Lara. *The Literary Invention of Margaret Cavendish*. Pittsburgh, PA: Duquesne University Press, 2013.

James, Susan, ed. *Margaret Cavendish: Political Writings*. Cambridge Texts in the History of Political Thought. New York: Cambridge University Press, 2003.

Larson, Katherine R. *Early Modern Women in Conversation*. New York: Palgrave Macmillan, 2011.

Malcolmson, Cristina. *Studies of Skin Color in the Early Royal Society: Boyle, Cavendish, and Swift*. Literary and Scientific Cultures of Early Modernity. Burlington, VT: Ashgate Publishing, 2013.

O'Neill, Eileen. "Early Modern Women Philosophers and the History of Philosophy." *Hypatia* 20 (2005): 185-97.

Rees, Emma L. E. *Margaret Cavendish: Gender, Genre, Exile*. New York: Manchester University Press, 2003

Sarasohn, Lisa T. *The Natural Philosophy of Margaret Cavendish: Reason and Fancy during the Scientific Revolution*. Baltimore, MD: Johns Hopkins University Press, 2010.

Siegfried, Brandie R. and Lisa T. Sarsohn, eds. *God and Nature in the Thought of Margaret Cavendish*. Burlington, VT: Ashgate Publishing, 2014.

Weise, Wendy S. "Recent Studies in Margaret Cavendish, Duchess of Newcastle (2001-2010)." *English Literary Renaissance* 42, no. 1 (2012): 146-76.

Appendix

A Brief Chronology of Margaret Cavendish's Published Work

This list includes the various names under which Margaret Cavendish published her work as well as each book's printer and bookseller as specified on title pages. It also includes all editions and reissues.

Poems, and Fancies, "written by the Right Honourable, the Lady Margaret Countess of Newcastle." London, 1653. Printed by T[homas] R[ycroft] for J[ohn] Martin and J[ames] Allestrye "at the Bell in Saint Pauls Church Yard."[1]

Philosophicall Fancies, "written by the Right Honourable, the Lady Newcastle." London, 1653. Printed by Tho[mas] R[y]croft for J[ohn] Martin and J[ames] Allestrye "at the Bell in St. Pauls Church-yard."

The Worlds Olio, "written by the Right Honorable, the Lady Margaret Newcastle." London, 1655. Printed for J[ohn] Martin and J[ames] Allestrye "at the Bell in St. Pauls Church-Yard."

The Philosophical and Physical Opinions, "written by her Excellency, the Lady Marchionesse of Newcastle." London, 1655. Printed for J[ohn] Martin and J[ames] Allestrye "at the Bell in St. Pauls Church-Yard."

---

[1] Cameron Kroetsch notes the existence of at least one different title page, this one omitting the reference to "countess" and simply attributing the book's authorship to "the Right Honourable, the Lady Newcastle." Kroetsch, "List of Margaret Cavendish's Texts, Printers, and Booksellers (1653-1675)," *Digital Cavendish Project* (2013), http://www.digitalcavendish.org/texts-printers-booksellers/.

Natures Pictures Drawn by Fancies Pencil to the Life. In This Volume There are Several Feigned Stories of Natural Descriptions, as Comical, Tragical, and Tragi-Comical, Poetical, Romancical, Philosophical, and Historical, Both in Prose and Verse, Some All Verse, Some All Prose, Some Mixt, Partly Prose, and Partly Verse. Also, There Are Some Morals, and Some Dialogues, But They Are as the Advantage Loaves of Bread to a Bakers Dozen, and a True Story at the Latter End, Wherein There is no Feignings, "written by the Thrice Noble, Illustrious, and Excellent Princess, the Lady Marchioness of Newcastle." London, 1656. Printed for J[ohn] Martin, and J[ames] Allestrye "at the Bell in Saint Paul's Church-yard."[2]

Playes, "written by the Thrice Noble, Illustrious and Excellent Princess, the Lady Marchioness of Newcastle." London, 1662. Printed by A[lice] Warren for John Mart[i]n, James Allestry[e], and Tho[mas] Dicas "at the Bell in Saint Pauls Church Yard."

Orations of Divers Sorts, Accommodated to Divers Places, "written by the Thrice Noble, Illustrious, and Excellent Princess, the Lady Marchioness of Newcastle." London, 1662.[3]

The Philosophical and Physical Opinions, written by "the Thrice Noble, Illustrious, and Excellent Princess, the Lady Marchioness of Newcastle." 2nd ed. London, 1663. Printed by William Wilson.[4]

CCXI Sociable Letters, written by "the Thrice Noble, Illustrious, and Excellent Princess, the Lady Marchioness of Newcastle." London, 1664. Printed by William Wilson.

---

[2] The title pages of *The Worlds Olio*, *Philosophical and Physical Opinions*, and *Natures Picture* list no printer, but Kroetsch suggests that the books were probably printed by Thomas Rycoft.

[3] Although the title page does not list a printer, Kroetsch indicates that the printer was William Wilson.

[4] According to Kroetsch (n15), "After 1662 the name of the bookseller does not appear on Cavendish's title pages. Since the remaining printers were not listed as being booksellers, it is possible that Allestrye, Martin, and Dicas continued to sell all of her books, or that at least Allestrye and/or Martin did. . . . Whitaker [*Mad Madge*] suggests that Margaret, at least by the time she is printing with Anne Maxwell, does not have the need for a large firm of booksellers, and arranges for printing and selling on her own (310)."

Poems and Phancies, "written by the Thrice Noble, Illustrious, and Excellent Princess the Lady Marchioness of Newcastle." 2nd ed., "much altered and corrected." London, 1664. Printed by William Wilson.

Philosophical Letters, or, Modest Reflections upon Some Opinions in Natural Philosophy, Maintained by Several Famous and Learned Authors of this Age, Expressed by Way of Letters, written by "the Thrice Noble, Illustrious, and Excellent Princess, the Lady Marchioness of Newcastle." London, 1664.[5]

Observations upon Experimental Philosophy, to Which is Added "The Description of a New Blazing World," written by "the Thrice Noble, Illustrious, and Excellent Princesse, the Duchess of Newcastle." London, 1666. Printed by A[nne] Maxwell.

The Life of the Thrice Noble, High, Puissant Prince William Cavendishe, Duke, Marquess, and Earl of Newcastle . . . , written by "the Thrice Noble, Illustrious, and Excellent Princess, Margaret, Duchess of Newcastle." London, 1667. Printed by A[nne] Maxwell.

De Vita et Rebus Gestis Nobilissima Principis, Guilielmi Ducis Novocastrensis, commentarii. Ab Excellentissima Principe, Margareta ipsius uxore sanctissima conscripti. . . . London, 1668. Printed by T[homas] M[ilbourne].[6]

Grounds of Naturall Philosophy, Divided into thirteen Parts, with an Appendix Containing Five Parts, a reissue, "much altered," of *Philosophical and Physical Opinions*, written by "the Thrice Noble, Illustrious, and Excellent Princess, the Duchess of Newcastle." London, 1668. Printed by A[nne] Maxwell.

Observations upon Experimental Philosophy, to Which is Added "The Description of a New Blazing World," written by "the Thrice Noble, Illustrious, and Excellent Princesse, the Duchess of Newcastle." 2nd ed. London, 1668. Printed by A[nne] Maxwell.

---

[5] Although no printer is listed, Kroetsch posits that the book was printed by David Maxwell, whose widow, Anne Maxwell, becomes Cavendish's printer.

[6] Walter Charleton's Latin translation of Cavendish's biography of her husband.

The Description of a New World, Called the Blazing-World, written by "the Thrice Noble, Illustrious, and Excellent Princesse, the Duchess of Newcastle." London, 1668. Printed by A[nne] Maxwell.

Plays, Never before Printed, written by "the Thrice Noble, Illustrious, and Excellent Princesse, the Duchess of Newcastle." London, 1668. Printed by A[nne] Maxwell.

Poems, or, Several Fancies in Verse, with the Animal Parliament, in Prose, written by "the Thrice Noble, Illustrious, and Excellent Princesse, the Duchess of Newcastle." 3rd ed. of *Poems and Fancies*. London, 1668. Printed by A[nne] Maxwell.

Orations of Divers Sorts, Accommodated to Divers Places, "written by the Thrice Noble, Illustrious, and Excellent Princess, the Lady Marchioness of Newcastle." 2nd ed. London, 1668.

Natures Pictures Drawn by Fancies Pencil to the Life. Being Several Feigned Stories, Comical, Tragical, Tragi-comical, Poetical, Romancical, Philosophi?cal, Historical, and Moral: Some in Verse, some in Prose; some Mixt, and some by Dialogues, written by "the Thrice Noble, Illustrious, and Most Excellent Princess, the Duchess of Newcastle." 2nd ed. London, 1671. Printed by A[nne] Maxwell.

The Worlds Olio, "written by the Thrice Noble, Illustrious, and Most Excellent Princess, the Duchess of Newcastle." 2nd ed. London, 1671. Printed by A[nne] Maxwell.

The Life of the Thrice Noble, High, Puissant Prince William Cavendishe, Duke, Marquess, and Earl of Newcastle. 2nd ed. London, 1675. Printed by A[nne] Maxwell.